JAM MASTER JAY

JAM MASTER JAY

the heart of hip hop

David E. Thigpen

POCKET STAR BOOKS

New York London Toronto Sydney Singapore

An *Original* Publication of MTV Books/Pocket Books

A Pocket Star Book published by
POCKET BOOKS, a division of Simon & Schuster, Inc.
1230 Avenue of the Americas, New York, NY 10020

Copyright © 2003 by David E. Thigpen

MTV Music Television and all related titles, logos, and
characters are trademarks of MTV Networks, a division of
Viacom International Inc.

ISBN: 0-7434-7694-8

First MTV Books/Pocket Books mass market paperback printing April 2003

10 9 8 7 6 5 4 3 2 1

POCKET STAR BOOKS and colophon are registered trademarks of
Simon & Schuster, Inc.

For information regarding special discounts for bulk purchases,
please contact Simon & Schuster Special Sales at 1-800-456-6798
or business@simonandschuster.com

Front cover photo courtesy of Corbis

Printed in the U.S.A.

The author would like to acknowledge the following people for generously lending their expertise and knowledge which helped make this book possible: Bill Adler, Dave Sirulnick, Chuck D, Phil Nelson, Jim Tremayne, Rick Rubin, DJ Hurricane, and a special thanks to Christopher John Farley, whose advice and friendship have been invaluable.

And finally, this book is dedicated to Veronica, for seeing me through; and to Mom and Dad and my brothers, for bringing me this far.

David E. Thigpen
January 2003

CONTENTS

JAY'S LEGACY

On the night of October 30, 2002, I was working late in my office at *Time* magazine when something disturbing flashed across my computer screen. While scrolling through the latest news postings on one of the music news wires—a wonderful way of procrastinating when there's real work to be done—my eyes froze when I saw these words: "Hip Hop Pioneer Jam Master Jay shot in Queens studio."

For seven years, from 1993 to 2000, I was a music reporter on the staff of *Time* magazine in New York City and I often saw Jay up close, performing with Run-DMC, striding through record industry parties, or indulging eager fans as he tried to down a meal in a restaurant.

The last time I remember seeing him was at the 1999 MTV Video Music Awards at the Metropolitan Opera House in Lincoln Center. Run-DMC's glory days had mostly faded by then, but their musical achievements still resonated powerfully. Near the end of the show the trio suddenly came bounding through the auditorium, dressed in their familiar black hats, gold chains, and leather jackets, as the strains of one of their greatest songs could be heard rising in the background. Jay and Run and DMC performed their signature hit, "Walk This Way," with more gusto than ever. It was as though they were re-energized facing a large audience again, and the excitement was flowing through them right into the crowd.

Jay took his position at a set of twin turntables that had appeared from nowhere and began scratching records, the sound he made famous. Then, Run-DMC was joined by the rock band Aerosmith and the enormously popular rap-rocker Kid Rock. The three groups, Run-DMC representing the 1980s, Aerosmith the 1970s, and Kid Rock the 1990s, put a brief history of modern music right before our eyes. In the background I could see Jay laughing and smiling. You could tell he was in the best place on earth right then and there was no place he'd rather be.

Jam Master Jay was one-third of what is possibly the most important rap group of all time: Run-DMC. Music fans knew him as the group's jovial dj, the legendary backbone of Run-DMC, who gave the group its musical personality. Run-DMC's up-from-the-pavement saga—from street-corner phenoms to worldwide musical stars—paralleled other great music stories, like the Beatles', Elvis's, or Bob Dylan's, and they helped trigger the cultural revolution that anybody who owns a radio or tv or has a teenager in the household is already well aware of: hip hop. Hip hop was the new rock and roll, and the biggest youth quake of the last twenty-five years, and Jam Master Jay was one of its catalysts. His death, if true, would be a terrible loss.

After seeing the headline on my computer screen, I immediately e-mailed a fellow journalist in Brooklyn to ask if she had heard the news. A short time later I received her e-mail: "It's true."

An hour later when I arrived at home and shared the news with my wife, the story was everywhere, not just on MTV News but on CNN, Fox, and the network affiliates, too. One station was running a live feed from New York, where a reporter and a cameraman were already on the scene. We settled in to watch the video footage—still hoping that somehow the initial reports were incorrect.

The weather was lousy in New York that night. A hard, cold rain had been falling throughout most of the day, and the images coming across the screen were dim. But as the camera swung around I could make out in the weak glow of the street lamps that a large crowd was gathering near the entrance to what must be the recording studio, along a busy street in the borough of Queens. Police tape had been strung up, and when the lights of the tv camera fell on a group of people huddled on the sidewalk I saw on their faces unmistakable dread. I recognized some of the faces: There were music executives, musicians, radio disc jockeys, even some of the other members of Run-DMC.

For the longest time there seemed to be mostly confusion and precious little solid information. The police were mum and no one on the scene knew anything more than there had been shots fired, and Jay had been hit. A few minutes later my stomach dropped when the camera suddenly turned its eye on the studio's rear door. Two workers from New York City's police department emerged and began making their way down the fire escape stairs carrying something heavy. When I looked closer I could see that it was a body bag; Jam Master Jay was being taken away.

The live coverage carried on but after that I was so disheartened that I turned off the tv and went to bed. It was a terribly sad night for anyone close to Jay, of course, but it was also a sad night for hip hop, and for anyone who believes that music and our musicians are important cultural treasures. The next day the front page of many newspapers around the country reported Jay's death, and Run-DMC's history was dutifully recapped, as though this was their end.

But death is never an end. It is only another beginning.

Run-DMC were iconic figures in hip hop music. Copies of their wardrobe—-the black hats and gold neck chains they faithfully wore—are on display in the hip hop exhibit of the Rock and Roll Hall of Fame Museum in Cleveland. And they were generally recognized as trailblazers of hip hop's success.

My job has been the kind of job I dreamed about when I was in college: *Time* magazine pays me a salary every week to observe and write about the world, and for several years I covered the music business close up. I have been a music fan since I was very small, and I have early memories of hearing my parents play records in our house—the Supremes, Bob Dylan, Burt Bacharach, Peter, Paul, and Mary, the Beatles. To this day I can still remember virtually every note and lyric on some of those albums.

When I joined *Time* magazine, I set out to learn as much about the music industry as possible. The record business attracts all manner of colorful and theatrical personalities who often make great stories. It is also an industry bursting with money and the allure of power. I learned very early that the business of selling records and the art of creating music, although tightly intertwined, could hardly be more different. Great artistry often goes unrewarded; mediocre artistry frequently earns millions of dollars. Sometimes the business elevates the wrong things. Still, the miracle of making music that possesses all the right things—artistry, integrity, poeticism—and connects with a large audience is a truly awesome thing. What is more amazing than watching an arena full of people held rapt by a single musical note?

Scientists and neurologists have said that music is perhaps the most powerful language of all. It has the power to travel directly from its source right into the central nervous system of a listener, pure and unencumbered, in a way that media like painting and film cannot. Ideas like that help you understand why armies have marching songs, and nations have national anthems. And most important, I began to see that music tells a lot about who we are. It reflects the national mood as accurately as a Gallup poll, and reaches deeper into the hearts of people, revealing their hopes and anxieties. This makes the musician a lightning rod of sorts, gathering forces and energy from the cultural air and transforming them into something the rest of us find beautiful and motivating. In another context the scholar Lionel Trilling once wrote something that can very much be applied to musicians, a statement that made me think of Jay: "The poet may be used as the barometer, but let us not forget that he is also part of the weather."

There could hardly have been a more exciting time to cover music than the late 1990s. The sound of change was in the air, and it was on people's lips. Hip hop, which had sprouted from the cracks in the pavement and then grew up around the crack vials strewn in America's inner cities, was on its way to overtaking rock and country as the nation's best-selling musical genre. Alternative rock, the child of punk, made a dizzyingly fast rise up the sales charts but would soon experience an even more abrupt fall, after Kurt Cobain's suicide stunned the world. There were all sorts of smaller but no less interesting musical offshoots, too: techno, neo-soul, trip-hop, heavy metal, ska, rave, neo-folk, house, kiddie pop, drum and bass, and more.

But none of them was richer than hip hop, which sprouted in a profusion of simultaneous directions: gangsta, bounce, hip hop soul, roots, and later rap-rock. Nothing seemed to capture the hungry imagination of youth like hip hop. With its rebellious posture and contempt for most social niceties, it packaged the sort of unshaped anger and insolence of teenagers quite nicely, especially those growing up in the golden shackles of affluent suburban complacency.

There were bigger cultural changes at work, too: All of the entertainment industries were attracting more attention than they ever had before. Fueled by the media's obsession with celebrity, the music business began producing stars who became familiar to the cultural mainstream, names that just a few years earlier might have been known only to serious music heads. Entertainment moved to the center of our culture, as Americans became disillusioned with institutions they had leaned on in the past: politics, government, family, even the church. People began investing their feelings in entertainment personalities.

The rapper and music executive Sean Combs, better known as Puff Daddy or P. Diddy, became a celebrity and highly visible figure. So did the West Coast producer Dr. Dre and his protégés. LL Cool J even got a role in a tv series, while the West Coast rapper Ice Cube began developing a strong career as a movie actor. The intensified attention was a double-edged sword. While it brought great wealth upon many lucky artists and executives, it also seemed to raise the stakes, as money always does. When Puffy and Notorious B.I.G. recorded a song called "Mo Money, Mo Problems," they were describing their own success and the problems it raised, but it was easy to see that their message had greater meaning. The music business has always held out the allure of instant riches and the illusion of democracy in a way that most of the other entertainment businesses do not. Write a hit song, become rich and famous, and you don't have to look like a model to do so. The industry became more edgy and impatient and occasionally aggressive.

As I got deeper inside the music world, I was often amazed and sometimes disappointed at what I saw. I recall seeing Tupac Shakur barely a week before he would die in a drive-by shooting in Las Vegas, as he circulated at an industry party in Manhattan telling people he had enough trouble in his life and was looking forward to turning over a new leaf. When his fellow rapper Notorious B.I.G. was shot and killed six months later, I remember how those deaths threw a threatening shadow over hip hop and raised questions, fair or not, that demanded answers: Were these deaths aberrations, the work of outsiders, or did they represent something about hip hop and the people who comprise it? If hip hop's greatest artists are not safe, then what does the music stand for? Or were these deaths in fact merely the same sad gun violence that intrudes into every realm of American life? Were they exactly the sort of all-too-common urban tragedies that many rappers have attacked in their lyrics?

Death has become an unwelcome but familiar presence in hip hop. When no arrests were made in either case, questions and doubts lingered, like buzzards circling overhead.

Those questions flooded back into my mind as I pored over the initial accounts of Jam Master Jay's death. Over the following days, daily newspapers and television news shows kept up the coverage, devoting hours of air time and gallons of ink to speculation and debate over this latest killing of a hip hop star. Although the facts were still far from clear, much of the early speculation centered on the supposition that Jam Master Jay's shooting had some connection to the East-West tensions that cast a dark cloud over hip hop in the late 1990s.

This hip hop war began as nothing more than a series of verbal affronts between people affiliated with Suge Knight's Death Row record label in Los Angeles and Sean Combs's Bad Boy record label in New York. It first seemed to be juvenile jousting of the "I'm better—no you're not" ilk. Then the imaginary seemed to become real as a series of shootings followed, culminating in the deaths of Tupac and Notorious B.I.G.

As I covered those shootings for *Time*, I noticed that there was a harsh, judgmental tone to the mainstream press coverage. The implication seemed to be that there was no difference between the gangsta lyrics of

Tupac and Notorious B.I.G. and their lifestyles. Sure it was sad that they got shot, the coverage implied, but hey, they must have done something to bring it on themselves.

That too was the subtext in much of the early coverage of Jay's death. A day or two later, some of his closest friends came forward to say that Jay was not a gangster. He led a life removed from the rough edges of street life and the bad side of the record business, they said. He came from the streets, all right, but the streets were not in him. He was a regular family man, they said, with a wife and a house. He didn't live in the ghetto. When he came home at night he took off his black fedora and gold chain. He sometimes spent Saturdays teaching kids in his old neighborhood how to play chess.

The figure portrayed in the media was not the real Jay.

Over the next few days it became clear to me that Jay's shooting had struck a nerve. The magnitude of the outpouring of grief was astonishing. His record company and his wife and children were inundated with messages of condolence, some from as far away as Australia, Japan, and Finland. For days fans made pilgrimages to the site of his death, leaving mementos and tokens in tribute. A wake attracted nearly a thousand visitors, and on the day of his funeral some 6,000 people pressed up against police barricades lining the streets to watch Jay's funeral procession pass by on its way to a Queens church. Michael Bloomberg, the mayor of New York City, made a personal contribution of $10,000 to a reward fund put up to capture Jay's murderer. The loss of Jay seemed to have carved a profound hole in the life of New York.

When I looked more closely into Jay's life, I too discovered that there was so much about Jay that did not fit the image the public has of hip hop musicians. He was raising three children. He had studied computer science in college before dropping out to pursue a music career. He was a chess player and a basketball fanatic and a scholar of modern music who could name just about any record, its label and artist. I knew that Jay's story went deeper than most newspapers and tv news shows had shown.

As I began to ask questions about him, a new image began to emerge that was far different from the cardboard gangsta cutout figure of the tabloid newspapers, or the sanctified image put forth by his record label. Almost like one of those Polaroid pictures that slowly develops before your eyes, I began to gather a better picture of who Jam Master Jay was. The questions I asked were not just for my own satisfaction, either. Understanding the meaning of Jay's life—his ups and downs, the struggles, the victories, the way he handled success and failure—would help me answer hot questions facing all of hip hop, and for that matter all of music: What does a life devoted to hip hop stand for? What kind of life did he lead? Is there something more meaningful to the music he made than what we see on the surface? Maybe there would be an answer in there too to the question of why was he killed? I also wanted to know, what did Jay accomplish, and what legacy does he leave to his family and to the world?

I decided to retrace Jay's steps, from his youth in the Queens neighborhood of Hollis to his busy years on the road with Run-DMC to his return to Queens and his last minutes in his recording studio. I would interview his friends and those closest to him, the record executives he worked with, his schoolteachers, his neighbors, his barber—everyone who knew Jay and whose lives he touched. I would walk the streets of Hollis that he walked, visit the hallways of his high school, stand in the street corner park where he first set up his turntable, and see the house that he grew up in. I would track down some of his oldest friends and capture their memories of him from the years before he became famous. I wanted as complete a picture as possible, to know all of his inspirations and losses and triumphs. Everyone who spoke reflected on Jay's big heart, on his abundant generosity, and on his easy self-confidence.

His rise was far from smooth. At any given point in his path he encountered dozens of possible pitfalls. But Jay had a special ability for finding open doors. Whenever one would shut behind him, he was always able to find another one ahead of him, and swing it wide open. Jay started off life with very little. The more I learned about him, the more astonished I became at how much he achieved in just thirty-seven years on this earth. And perhaps most impressive of all is how little he changed. Even when the fruits of success were tumbling into his lap, he remained the same generous person that he was when he had nothing but a turntable and a dream. In adversity he was the same person as he was in victory, a sure sign of an exceptionally solid character.

As I write this, shortly after New Year's Day 2003, the record industry is still recoiling from Jay's death. No arrest has yet been made in his murder. In late 2002 the record industry ran into problems of its own, and appears to be teetering toward one of the most serious crises in recent memory. With sales down 13 percent from the preceding year, executives at the Big Five record companies—BMG, Universal, Sony, Warner Music, and EMI-Capitol—are bordering on panic. Most analysts blame it on lousy records, as well as losses due to Internet piracy.

The only bright spot in an otherwise down year were sales of hip hop records: three of the top ten best sellers were hip hop albums, and the biggest seller of the year was, like last year, a rap record. This year it was Eminem's *The Eminem Show*. Much of the blame can be laid at the foot of the record bosses themselves. For a decade the gatekeepers at the record labels have devoted more and more of their attention and resources into marketing only the most sensationalistic and visceral types of music—especially gangsta rap and hardcore metal. The traditional record company practice of developing new artists and giving them time to find an audience has been largely discarded in favor of a string of replaceable artists who may deliver one or two quick hits, then disappear. Faltering audience allegiance should come as no surprise then to an industry that works this way.

Times have changed, but maybe music executives ought to look back at Jay's career for some guidance. There's a lesson there, that music from the streets can endure, and have meaning beyond the purely visceral, yet still hold respect.

There are many more such lessons in Jay's life: Some people may argue that his death is a tragedy that gives hip hop a black eye. But his story is just as much—or more so—a message of how much good one person can do in a short time, and how much good one can leave behind.

one

LAST DAY ON EARTH

> "We're going to be together forever. We'll
> be 60 and performing Vegas."
>
> —DMC

It's tantalizing to imagine Jam Master Jay and his band mates Joseph "Run" Simmons and Darryl "DMC" McDaniels a decade or more from now still sporting their famous black hats and gold neck chains, performing their hits and relishing the sort of lucrative years that come to a tiny percentage of groups whose popularity manages to survive from one decade to the next. There would be a place of honor for them in the Rock and Roll Hall of Fame. There would be sold-out reunion tours and MTV specials. There would be screaming fans once again. And there would be big money pouring in.

Music is customarily thought of as a relentlessly youth-obsessed business, controlled by executives barely over thirty years old who spend their days and nights figuring out ways to market performers barely beyond adolescence. Mostly, this is true. But there's more to it than that. A group's professional twilight years can be the most profitable of all for both them and their record company. There's a giant sweet spot in the music market, right where nostalgia and clever promotion intersect. In 2002, some forty years after he first appeared on a record, Paul McCartney became the world's highest-earning touring act, grossing $103 million during a year when the ex-Beatle turned sixty years old. Billy Joel and Elton John, both in their fifties and on the downslope of their careers, toured together in the summer of 2001, pulling in a fee of $1 million per night. In October 2002, Run-DMC was well on its way to consolidating its fame into the sort of marketable formula that would pay out for years to come. 2002 had been a busy year; the trio performed about ten live shows every month, keeping them on the road two out of every three weeks. But the road was very good to them. They sometimes earned as much as $70,000 per night. $30,000 nights were not uncommon. Their current tour with the 1970s rock band Aerosmith and the 1990s rap-rocker Kid Rock was selling well and drawing good reviews.

This was an especially lucrative time for Jam Master Jay. Besides the Run-DMC tour he also had an array of side businesses that kept him running. Jay was one of the most famous dj's in the world, and in demand at nightclubs, parties, conventions, even art galleries and poetry slams. He often flew from a Run-DMC concert directly to a gig in another state, where he'd spin his records and then fly back again on the first plane out.

Then there was his record label. Early that fall he had signed a contract with Virgin Records, making them partners. As part of the deal, Jay would find promising young musicians and produce their records. For its part Virgin would promote and distribute those records. Jay and Virgin would each get a piece of any profits. For Virgin the value of the deal came from the benefit of having a respected dj finding talent and delivering it to them. For Jay it meant he could pocket a producer's fee for his work and not have to worry about the risk and expense of promoting and marketing a new act. Jay named his label Hot Ta Def Records, street slang for hot product, and he selected an unknown rap duo called Rusty Waters to be the label's first release.

One of the members of Rusty Waters was a man named Boe Skagz, who happened to be the son of Jay's sister Bonita, and the other was an old friend, Randy Allen. By late October Jay and Rusty Waters had the record mostly ready to go, except for a few finishing touches. Virgin hoped to have the record in stores by early 2003, so Jay was anxious to finish work on it and deliver it to the record company. On the night of Tuesday, October 29, after performing a dj gig in Birmingham, Alabama, Jay left early and caught a flight back to New York. He was looking forward to spending the night at home with his wife, Terri, and his three sons, Jason, Terry, and Jesse. Time was tight: He would spend most of Wednesday night in the studio, go home, and leave the next day to fly down to Washington, D.C., where Run-DMC was scheduled to perform at the half-time show of the season opener of the Washington Wizards basketball game, the team part-owned by Michael Jordan.

On Wednesday, October 30, Jay said goodbye to Terri and left the house in his SUV to visit a friend, run some errands, and make plans for that evening's session in the studio. Around 3 P.M. he came into Suge's barbershop in Queens off Merrick Boulevard and sat in his customary spot, the second chair from the window, which happens to be the best chair in the house, because it belongs to the shop's owner, Big Suge. When I visited Suge's in December, shortly after Jay was shot, the owner, Mike Vegas, was there wearing a white t-shirt, a black baseball cap, and a gold dog-tag-like medallion. He was still reeling. Suge's barbershop is the kind of place that is packed with fathers and sons waiting for a haircut, but the mood was somber on this day. Eventually the talk turned to Jay. "He'd been around and was full of wisdom," says Vega. "When I was in seventh grade I remember seeing him sitting on top of a Cadillac outside of school. He was my idol then. We became friends. He'd come in and sit down and we'd talk about football or he'd give me advice." That day he gave Jay his customary haircut, a Caesar fade, and Jay tried to help Suge navigate through some female problems. Jay said good-bye and stopped at the deli a few doors away to pick up a sandwich.

Later, Jay and his assistant and old friend Darnell Smith met another Hollis friend, Garfield McDonald, and they went shopping on the avenue, the central shopping area of that part of Queens. Jay bought some records, then announced that he was going up to the studio to work on some tracks. Garfield considered going up to the studio with Jay for a moment, then said goodbye to his old friend and headed home. Randy Allen would go in ahead of him and make preparations on the sound boards for the Rusty Waters project. Jay arrived at the studio as it was getting dark outside, parking his SUV nearby. It was raining that night, so he hurried inside. Around Queens, Jay's studio—formally known as "Studio 24/7"—is so famous that it is known simply as "the studio." Everybody knew when they'd see Jay's big black SUV parked outside that he was in there working.

Jay was in a great mood. He was looking forward to the D.C. trip the next day, and Virgin Records had recently told him that they were enthusiastic about the Rusty Waters tracks they had heard so far. Jay had also just produced some of the first recordings of a fast-rising new Queens rapper named Curtis Jackson, better known by the stage name 50 Cent. Things were going well on a personal level with Run-DMC, too. After a few rough years where they had all but drifted apart, the trio was back touring again and his old pals Run and DMC were both in good places in their lives. DMC had dried out, beat his drinking problem, and become a health nut. Run was an ordained minister and he had remarried happily.

Jay settled into the studio and began playing a video game while he waited for Randy to finish preparing the board. The studio is divided into two rooms: the engineering room and studio itself, and an outer lounge with couches for guests to relax and a desk and a computer where Jay's assistants handle the studio bookkeeping. There is a large tv screen in the lounge, too, and a couple of video game control boards. Jay liked nothing better than to unwind with a video game. The other people present that night were Randy, his sister Lydia High, who functions as a business partner for Jay, Boe Skagz, Mike B, a friend whom Jay was allowing to crash in the studio while he looked for his own place, and Uriel Rincon, another assistant. Around 7 P.M. someone came to the studio with a demo tape asking Jay to listen to it. Jay said he couldn't right now, he was busy, but leave the tape there and he would listen to it later. It was not unusual for aspiring musicians to seek Jay's support and opinion on demos—Jay often allowed friends and friends of friends to use the studio for free to get their ideas down on tape. Who knew, maybe there was a hit in there somewhere. On that night, though, Randy volunteered to give the tape a listen.

To get into Studio 24/7 you have to pass through an outer door that faces Merrick Boulevard, ring a bell and get buzzed through a second door, climb a stairwell, and pass through one last door, which is usually locked. The studio shares the entranceway with two other small businesses, so it is possible to get buzzed in simply by pressing one of the other bells. A security camera watches the entranceway, but on October 30 it had been out of order for at least a couple of months.

Jay never seemed concerned about his security. Everyone knew him in the neighborhood, and he was so well liked that whenever he stopped to talk to an old friend on the street, a crowd would quickly gather and he'd find himself signing autographs and pocketing cassette tapes shoved at him by high school kids eager to become rappers. And besides, this was his home turf, the place where he grew up, and the place where he had survived all the hard knocks kids coming up in the rougher parts of Queens face. Fistfights, gunshots—he had come through it all. The studio was his oasis.

Just before 7:30 P.M. a man, over six feet tall and wearing a pullover cap, somehow got into the building. Jay and Rincon were sitting in the lounge locked in a close game of video football. The man climbed the stairs. In his hand was a .40-caliber pistol. Jay and Rincon continued playing their football game. Randy and Boe were in the back room of the studio still making preparations. Lydia was seated closest to the door. The man with the gun was outside the door now and pulling his hat down over his face. He was checking his gun. Lydia opened the door when she heard a knock. The man was in the studio now and he was firing.

Jam Master Jay didn't come home that night.

two

I REMEMBER HOLLIS

To know where Jason came from, you first need to understand Hollis.

To followers of rap music, Hollis, Queens, will forever be remembered in the same way Liverpool, England, is honored by rock fans as the launching pad for the Beatles, or the way rhythm and blues fans revere Detroit, Michigan, as the cradle of soul music.

Hollis lies about thirty minutes east of Manhattan in the southeast corner of Queens, bordered by the neighborhood of Jamaica, which is the center of African-American Queens, and St. Alban's and Cambria Heights. People who have never visited New York often imagine that the entire city looks like the images they see on 1970s police shows—a blur of neon signs, high-rise buildings, tenements, and choking traffic. But in fact, once you leave the concrete canyons of Manhattan the sky opens up and miles and miles of low-rise office buildings, shops, apartments, and single-family houses stretch out before you.

A month after Jay passed I drove to Hollis to have a look. As you approach Hollis from the west, large brick houses give way to smaller two-story frame homes, each with a driveway and a postage-stamp-sized front yard. Many of the houses appear in need of a little sprucing up. At the intersection of Hollis Avenue and Francis Lewis Boulevard, one of the neighborhood's busiest corners, there is a deli grocery, a couple of beauty salons, a meat shop, a hardware store, two gas stations, and a donut shop. Mostly, the neighborhood looks as if it's seen better days, and it has.

Hollis was named by Frederick Dunton, a Queens real estate developer who bought 136 acres of farmland there in 1885 and named it after his hometown in New Hampshire. From the 1920s until just after World War II, hundreds of tract houses sprang up. By the 1950s Hollis was known as a stable, middle-class suburb of Manhattan, a place where cramped dwellers of sunlight-free tenements in the Bronx and Brooklyn aspired to settle. With its three-bedroom houses, many of them replete with family rooms, finished basements, and front yards that sprouted fruit trees, Hollis was populated by educators, small business owners, city bureaucrats, and insurance men. As a schoolboy in the 1940s, Secretary of State Colin Powell moved from the Bronx to Hollis with his family. He later fondly recalled in his memoirs that "the neighborhood looked beautiful to us, and the Hollis address carried a certain cachet." Powell's father reveled in his new status. "Our new home was ivy-covered, well kept and comfortable," Powell writes, "and had a family room and a bar in a finished basement. Pop was now a property holder, eager to mow his postage-stamp lawn and prune his fruit trees. My father had joined the gentry."

Queens became a fertile ground for musicians. Hollis later became an artistic hotbed of sorts. Besides producing all three members of Run-DMC, Hollis and its surrounding area can claim an illustrious list of achievers who were either born there or moved there: the rappers LL Cool J and Q-Tip; hip hop's foremost entrepreneur and record executive, Russell Simmons (and older brother of Run); FUBU apparel company founder Daymon John; rapper Ja Rule; as well as the popular NYC radio dj Ed Lover and the Hollywood actor Joe Morton. Hollis's fame even surpassed that of the nearby St. Alban's neighborhood, which was home to the great singer Sarah Vaughan and, for a time, Count Basie. Just a few miles away in Corona you can find the home where Louis Armstrong lived for the last decade of his life. Hollis itself has a unique combination of big-city hustle and small-town, neighborly vibe that still exists to this day. Passersby greet each other on the street, and just about everyone seems to know everyone else. Many of the residents have lived there for decades, often in the same house. Neighbors keep an eye on each other's property and strangers roaming the blocks draw curious glances.

Hollis changed rapidly in the early 1970s. Spurred

by rising inflation and sinking real estate prices, the neighborhood slid into economic decline, forcing many once-prosperous homeowners to turn their homes into rooming houses, and business storefronts were turned into bargain and discount shops. Hollis remained integrated through most of the 1960s, but in the 1970s accelerating white flight changed its complexion permanently. As more and more African-Americans moved in, whites moved away to the outer suburbs of Long Island. Russell Simmons remembered that the block his family lived on was a lively mix of whites and blacks until the early 1970s, when, in what seemed like a matter of a few weeks, all the white families moved out. In the 1980s Caribbean immigrants joined African-Americans in the migration into Hollis. But the most disruptive social change had nothing to do with immigration or housing patterns. Crack cocaine swept through New York City in the early 1980s, establishing a violent and highly profitable street trade that would hang on for nearly a decade. Its impact was felt on the streets of Hollis. "Growing up in Hollis, we had a choice," Russell Simmons remembered in a 1986 interview with *New York* magazine. "We could either stay on our block, which was nice, or you could go to the corner, which was like the corner in the Bronx or any other neighborhood. Two blocks from us was a big heroin block when we grew up. Now there's a crack corner."

Crack took a very visible toll on every neighborhood where it got a foothold: With crack came guns, and many of those guns wound up in the hands of young people, which made the streets of Hollis more like the rest of New York City. Hollis's days as a place where an aspiring middle class hoped to come and find a peaceful life were over. Still, some of the old neighborhood vibe remained. "Growing up in Hollis was special," Run remembered in his autobiography, *It's Like That*. "Nice homes, manicured yards and everything. But it wasn't like we were sheltered from the world." Dj's from the Bronx would later accuse dj's from Queens of being soft and suburban and therefore not as authentic as the rap musicians who hailed from housing projects. It probably wasn't fair, but it would become a sore spot for Run-DMC and Jason. "It's no matter where you're from," Jason told writer Bill Adler in *Tougher than Leather: The Rise of Run-DMC*: "It's who you are. There's no difference between the Bronx and Queens. It's just that we live in houses and they live in projects. So what? They went outside and had a fight with the guy down the block. We went outside and had a fight with the guy around the corner. No difference. Everything that was everywhere else was in Queens, too."

Jesse and Connie Mizell moved to Hollis from Brooklyn in 1975 with their three children, Marvin, Bonita, and Jason. When she first met Jesse Mizell, Connie already had two children from her late first husband. Marvin had been born in 1955, and then Bonita in 1958. Jesse was a social worker. Connie attended night school, worked as an assistant teacher for a couple of years, and then taught first grade full-time in a Brooklyn public school. The Mizells were excited to be escaping Brooklyn and coming to the relative spaciousness of Hollis. Jesse in particular loved his new home and spent hours tidying up the property and tinkering with things inside the house.

Jason William Mizell, their youngest child, was born January 21, 1965. Everyone always said he bore a strong resemblance to his mother, and when his mother looked at him, it was as though she saw a light coming from him. Being the youngest, Jason got plenty of attention. Jason displayed a strong musical inclination from an early age. When he was five he began playing drums and singing in the choir at his parents' church, Universal Baptist in Brooklyn. The Mizells' home in Hollis was a three-bedroom house at 109-83 203rd Street, two stories, with powder-gray aluminum siding, a sheltered front porch, and a low stone wall separating the front yard from the sidewalk. Jason's bedroom was on the second floor. His half-brother Marvin, who works as a driver for Greyhound, and his half-sister Bonita, who works for New York City social service agencies, still live there.

The Mizell house was always impeccably orderly, and there was never a time when there wasn't something cooking in the kitchen. Connie always had something hot ready and on the table for Jason before he left the house in the morning, and she usually greeted Jason's friends like this: "Hey baby, how are you doing?

You want something to eat?" Jason's close pal Darnell Smith remembers that "you could tell where Jason got his upbringing from. Jason's mom was real nice and laid back. She was the favorite neighborhood mom. And she let Jason make his own decisions." Connie had high standards, perhaps picked up from her own father, who raised a family working as a sharecropper, and watched his daughter go on to become a teacher, which for Southern laborers in the first half of the twentieth century was just as good as becoming a doctor. Connie expected her son to dress well, speak clearly, and always be punctual. They had high hopes for Jason and always let him know that they stood behind him. The Mizells are a strong, tightly knit family. Every Memorial Day, rain or shine, they drive south to Ahoskie, North Carolina, where Connie's family hails from, for a family reunion. Jason always came along, and even brought some of his Hollis friends occasionally. Those reunions would sometimes draw together fifty or more members of the Mizell clan, who'd spend the weekend sitting in lawn chairs, barbecuing ribs and reminiscing. When Jason later made money as a dj, he sent his mom to live in North Carolina, where the streets are safer and the air is cleaner than in Queens.

Jason attended Junior High School 192 on Hollis Avenue just a few blocks away from his home. His favorite class was music, which was a brave choice because among Hollis seventh, eighth, and ninth graders, musical skill could cause harm to your reputation. Most of the tough kids at 192 thought music was soft and refused to set foot in the instrument room. But Jason joined the thirty other students there anyway, even though when he looked around himself, he saw the room was heavily sprinkled with nerds. Jason started off on the tuba, which no one else wanted to play, and then switched to trombone. After a while he finally worked his way up to the coolest instrument in the school: the drums. Jason and his classmates always paid close attention and stayed out of trouble in music class because their teacher had a habit of tossing his music stand across the room when he got upset.

Jay was a natural musician, and he got plenty of encouragement from his teacher. He later added bass guitar to his repertoire and began experimenting with keyboards. And after a while, the idea of being a musician didn't seem so bad anymore. In fact, it was cool. "Back then you were either into music, you were a ballplayer, or you were a gangster," remembers Bruce Alan Bishop, who grew up in Hollis a few years ahead of Jason. "Those were the only tickets out." Jason may not have yet been thinking about a ticket out of the neighborhood, but he had found something he was good at, and it would continue to become a bigger part of his life.

In 1980 he entered Andrew Jackson High, a massive C-shaped tan brick building that was opened in 1936 and had changed very little in the intervening years. With long, cavernous hallways, shiny floors, and ancient, heavy wood doors, it has a fortress-like appearance, as if it was built to withstand a tank attack. Today

Jackson has been renamed Campus Magnet School, and as you enter the imposing front doors you are greeted by three uniformed New York City Police Department school safety officers with walkie-talkies. Next to their desk sits an airport-style metal detector. Jackson drew from a wide area of southeastern Queens and crammed 3,400 students in its hallways and classrooms during the 1970s and 1980s. "It was like a lot of high schools are today," says the radio dj Ed Lover, who once worked there as a security guard. "It was a little crazy at times, just high school kids trying to find their way. Everybody wanted to have the latest new thing, whatever that was. Everybody was trying to be cool." But there were so many teachers and so many classrooms that class sizes were manageable—usually about thirty to forty kids. Jay was bright but not diligent, a good enough student to hang out with the nerds when he wanted to, but too cool to get labeled with the scarlet "N." Sara Furtado worked as a paraprofessional at Jackson High in the late 1970s and remembers Jason as a lively personality with a quick wit. "He was a rambunctious kid, but not a bad kid," she told me. "He was spirited and a lot of fun."

In Claude Brown's unforgettable memoir of growing up in New York City, *Manchild in the Promised Land,* he describes a Harlem neighborhood in the 1950s that would not have seemed unfamiliar to Hollis kids in the late 1970s. "As I saw it in my childhood, most of the cats I swung with were more afraid of not fighting than they were of fighting. This was how it was supposed to be, because this was what we had come up under." At Jackson, Jason quickly realized that there were bigger, tougher kids who applied themselves to fighting and intimidation the same way other students apply themselves to studying. Jackson was divided up into three large groups of kids—the Hollis kids, the Southside kids, and the Five Percenters, Muslims who were an offshoot of the Nation of Islam. Although they weren't gangs in the sense that we know them today— that is, wearing the same colors and intimidating whole neighborhoods—bands of Jackson kids never-theless operated en masse, roaming the hallways in packs and hanging around the school grounds to-gether. "I was tough enough to protect my lunch money," Jason once told a reporter, but marauding groups of bigger kids made walking on the wrong side of the hallway between classes potentially unhealthy. So, Jason mastered the art of making friends—and al-lied himself with some of the biggest and toughest kids in the school.

One of Jason's first friends was Wendell Fite, who would later make a name for himself as DJ Hurricane, the dj for the white hip hop group the Beastie Boys. One day a brawl between two posses of students broke out in the school hallway and one poor soul had gotten backed into corner and was taking a mighty beating. Suddenly the boy in the corner pulled out a handgun and fired a shot into the ceiling. As the crowd scattered another shot went wild. Jason and Hurricane were in the crowd and turned to run, but Hurricane took a few steps, felt a stinging in his leg, and fell. He tried to run again, but again he stumbled. When he looked down at his left leg he saw blood; he had been shot, and the kid with the gun was now coming toward him. "Nobody noticed I was hit. Everybody else was gone down the hall and I'm lying there with this guy coming at me and then I look up and I see Jason. He came back and lifted me up and dragged me out of there. We were friends forever from there on out."

But first they had to avenge the shooting. When they learned that the shooter—who had already been sent to jail—was a member of the Five Percenters, Hurricane's pals delivered beat-downs to any and all Five Percenters they could find. In a few weeks the Five Percenters were vanquished as a force at Jackson High.

Jason, Hurricane, and their pals—"the Hollis crew," as they came to be called—soon exercised dominion over the school. "We were like an army," Hurricane reminisced. "If you fought one of us you fought all of us. It was stupid teenage stuff, but that's the way it was." Once when another kid punched Jason in the nose, several Hollis guys made sure it would never happen again. Like any conquering force, the victors demanded tribute. So, whenever lunchtime would roll around, Hurricane and other Hollis crew members posted themselves at the entrance to the lunchroom. If you wanted to enter to get a sandwich and glass of milk you had to pay them two dollars. If you couldn't pay, you were out of luck. At the end of each day the Hollis crew would have enough money to buy beer—Olde

English 800—and cigarettes—Old Gold charcoal filtered—and any other spoils of war they desired. And Jason got respect. "Everybody respected Jason after that," remembers Hurricane. "If you messed with Jason you had a big problem. He was the top dog in school. Nobody touched him."

Jason had very quickly emerged as someone everyone wanted to be friends with. He was the coolest kid in school. Soon he could be seen around Jackson with a knot of followers trailing him. His reputation spread around the neighborhood, and even some of the older kids wanted to hang out with him. On weekends Jason sometimes led a crew of friends into Manhattan, where they would catch a movie or try to sneak into one of the new hip hop clubs in Harlem or downtown Manhattan. Jason and his crew made quite a sight, piling onto a subway car ten or twenty strong and occupying a whole row of benches as the stations whizzed past and other riders avoided eye contact. When they arrived at their destination, Jason always made sure everyone in his posse got inside, even if he had to hold the fire door open himself. Jason also began experimenting with his wardrobe, trying on different hats, oversized belt buckles, leather jackets. He was just a teenager, but he seemed to instinctively understand that a leader has to dress the part, too. The beginnings of what would become Run-DMC's famous attire started in Jason's experiments back in high school, as he tried to find a look that would let the world know that he was cool.

School and academics, however, were quickly losing their charm for him. "I was smarter than everybody in my class all the time," he said to *Rolling Stone*, "so I just felt like I didn't have to do the work. I was going to school, but I was messing up in school." And the stress of the frequent fights, the occasional gunshots, and having to watch his back all the time added up. He began thinking of getting out. He would often sit in the back in class and imagine himself playing drums in a hot band and touring the world. He imagined himself becoming famous and returning to Hollis and watching as every girl in the neighborhood fawned over him. He imagined driving a big car and getting on planes and seeing the world, all things that seemed so impossibly far away, and so out of reach. In his junior year, worn down by the stress and bored by classes, he dropped out of Jackson. Many of his friends did the same. Over the course of the next year Jason completed a GED to keep his parents happy. But now that he was out of school, he was gravitating rapidly toward the streets and away from everything else.

There was a perverse appeal in street life: You could guzzle beer in the middle of the day, you never really had to be anywhere on a schedule, the conversation was usually bawdy and entertaining, and if you played your cards right, there was money in it. There was an odd level of respect you received, and people stuck in their dull 9-to-5 jobs gave the street guys a wide berth. There was always a bustling street scene in Hollis, hanging outside one of the corner delis or outside the barbershop, where a steady flow of foot traffic kept things lively. When cash was short you panhandled from passersby. But hanging out with the crew on Hollis Avenue was also a prescription for trouble. Before long, Jason got involved with whatever petty crime his pals were into—thefts, chain snatchings, pickpocketing. "We were in our early teens and we were doing bad teenager stuff," says Hurricane. "We were just acting out." Most of the crimes they pulled off were not because they were starving or in need of a new coat. They did it because they were bored and saw people with nice things that they didn't have. Connie and Jesse Mizell heard stories about their son running the streets of Hollis, but they continued giving Jason all their unconditional support, even as their worries about the company he was keeping grew deeper.

Once he became a regular on the street corner, Jason came under peer pressure to go along with the group. The stress, he was learning, was even worse than sitting around all day in a Jackson High classroom. His heart was not in pulling off crimes on the street, but he had a reputation to look after, and sometimes that required doing things that he knew weren't right. One day it finally landed him in jail. When he was fifteen a friend of his staged a burglary of a doctor's house and made a clean getaway, or so he thought. Jason was not in on the burglary but he turned up afterward to see what the take was. As his friend was showing off the loot an undercover cop appeared and gave chase. Jason ran one way and his friend another. Maybe it was because he was slower, but the cop came after Jason. The friend escaped. Jason got caught and was hauled down to the police precinct. But he was too ashamed to tell his parents what had happened, so he refused to tell the cop where he lived. After a long wait in the precinct, the cop figured that Jason was underage, and sent him to juvenile jail for holding.

Jason wound up spending four days in Spofford, the tough Bronx juvenile facility that is a way station for many future long-term guests of the New York State penal system. Spofford had a bad reputation even among hardened Hollis kids, and deservedly so. It was a Riker's Island for kids, full of some of the toughest hombres in New York City. Spofford is an imposing grim-looking facility where inmates are held in cells with heavy steel doors instead of bars, and there are guards everywhere to prevent troubled kids from hurting each other. But Spofford turned out to be far less frightening than Jason had expected. "Pool table, ping pong, and basketball in the backyard," he told writer Bill Adler. Jason even recognized some faces from the streets of Hollis there. "All in all when my pops picked me up I was having a really good time," he said. At first he was impressed with himself, proud that he had gone into such a bad place and come out unscathed. But later as he looked back, he realized that fitting in at a place like Spofford made him stupid, not smart.

As for his parents, when they found out where he had been, and what his reaction was to his little unscheduled vacation, they were positively crushed. When he got home and walked in the front door his mother began to cry. Everything she had taught him seemed to have been lost. Instead of her bright son, she saw a future criminal. She saw her hopes crashing to the ground right in front of her. Jason saw the tears and instantly realized how much he had hurt his mother. Said Jason: "That's when I changed completely. I got the idea that you didn't have to rob and steal to be the best and have the most juice." He later admitted to *Rolling Stone* that "I stopped being wild when I was 16. When I say wild, I just didn't care." He decided to retire from street life and find something with a future. He set out in a new direction: He took a string of odd jobs so he could get a little cash in his pocket without having to hustle on the streets. First he worked as a telemarketer, and then as a security guard at Columbia University in upper Manhattan, patrolling the perimeter of student dorms from 12 A.M. to 6 A.M., the graveyard shift. Those long, still hours and the lousy pay made him wonder where his life was going, and if it was going anywhere.

Jason was on a less risky track but everything in his life was about to change in an even bigger way. In 1982 Jesse Mizell fell ill. Jason spent a few weeks at home caring for his father, but in October, Jesse passed away. Connie was beside herself, but Jesse's death hit Jason even harder. His older brother Marvin was already living outside of the house, so Jason became the man of the household, comforting his mom and sister and taking on more responsibility. He remembered all the encouragement his dad had given him and he wondered if he had let him down. He began to rethink everything. "After my father died I really wised up," he said in *Rolling Stone*. "Everything changed for me then." He suddenly felt that there was precious little time to waste—that life was slipping past him and if he didn't do something quick, he might wind up like the wild-eyed guys he saw hanging out on Hollis Boulevard who have been in the same spot every day for the last five years. Jason decided that he would focus seriously on his music for a while to see where it would take him. He began spending increasingly larger amounts of time practicing drums, first in his room and then later, when he accumulated more equipment, down in the basement. Eventually there was a parade of friends in and out of the Mizell house as Jason began practicing with other kids and talking about forming their own band. Soon he would get his first turntable and all that would change. Once more, Connie was nothing but supportive. As Jason became more engrossed in making music, he spread his equipment from one end of the house to another.

Every day Connie would come home from school, see the mess, and say, that's ok. That's alright.

three

HIP HOP CRUCIBLE

In the beginning there was the dj, and the noise he made was def.

For teenagers accustomed to filling their spare time shooting basketball and staging rip-offs and assorted petty crimes, the first appearance of hip hop in the late 1970s sent currents of excitement pulsing through Hollis. "It's like basketball," Jason said a few years later, describing his feelings when he saw his first dj and heard his first rap song. "As soon as it comes to your neighborhood you want to know how to do it; you want to be with it." It's difficult to determine the exact moment of hip hop's birth (1975 is as close a date as any), but it is widely agreed that the loosely connected bundle of street art forms—break dancing, graffiti writing, rapping, and deejaying—the four fundamental elements of hip hop culture—first appeared together in the Bronx. Very soon thereafter they cropped up in Harlem, Queens, and Brooklyn. In the early 1980s all four elements spread virally around the city. Hollis's location—just past the outer edge of the city's subway lines—meant that hip hop's hot spots were never more than a fifty-cent subway ride away. Any new trend popping up in Harlem or the Bronx on a Friday night usually turned up in Hollis a day or two later, transported by subway and bus.

The first wave of hip hop was almost entirely under-ground—meaning that it had no commercial life what-soever, and existed below the radar of record companies. Run described those early days in his autobiography this way: "Hip hop was something that happened on the playgrounds, in parks, and at parties. There was no big money. There were no movie deals, record contracts, or endorsements." But the music was not the first element of hip hop to spread itself around. Break dancing, with its visual spectacle of whirling limbs and acrobatic gyra-tions, spread the quickest, popping up almost instantly in parks and later nightclubs throughout New York City. By the early 1980s it became a common sight to see teenage boys carrying flattened cardboard boxes around the streets, which, when spread out on the ground, turned any surface—be it an asphalt playground or sub-way platform—into an instant dance floor. The very first hip hop–influenced films—*Beat Street* and *Breaking* (both released in 1984)—let the camera's eye linger ad-miringly on the break dancers, as if it were anticipating that they were destined to become the new culture's first stars. But that never happened. Break dancers got a little free publicity in 1980 when one of the city's first loosely organized troupes, the High Times crew, were arrested for dancing in the subway. But break dancing never could muster the staying power needed to break into the mass consciousness and it never grew into a widely accepted art form. There would be sporadic revivals, but break dancing would finally end up in the retirement home for unwanted trends, alongside the Lambada and the Macarena.

Many thought at the time that graffiti artists would attract and hold fame. After all, in many ways they were the most romanticized figures in early hip hop culture: lone figures with a renegade streak and an artistic bent, armed with nothing but a spray can. Set loose in New York, they boldly imagined the physical city itself as their canvas. But graffiti gained even less momentum than break dancing, and would remain, with a few exceptions, an underground art form. One reason is that in the middle 1980s New York launched a crackdown on graffiti, after deciding it had a negative impact on "quality of life." Several of the top graffiti artists were caught and arrested by the New York City Police Department, which had scant appreciation for graffiti as art. A couple of graffiti writers even lost their lives, like Michael Stewart, a young Brooklyn man whom police collared on a subway platform in the wee hours of a September morning in 1983, spray can in hand. During the arrest a struggle of some sort broke out and Stewart took quite a beating: By the time he was brought to the hospital he was in a coma. A week later he died. Another reason why graffiti artists never escaped the underground is that rather surprisingly, one of the most elitist institutions in the city very alertly reached down and stole their thunder. By the early 1980s the fine art world was embracing and paying good money to the painter Jean-Michel Basquiat and the illustrator Keith Haring, two artists whose work reflected their early years roaming the streets and scrawling their marks wherever they could. Break dancing and graffiti could never find a commercial base to build on, and were destined to remain underground. They very quickly receded, and today seem like curiously distant artifacts of a bygone era.

The words hip hop gradually became synonymous with rap—that is, signifying the music alone. From a very early point, then, music seemed to be where the soul of hip hop lived. And the rappers and dj's who were inventing it as they went along had no trouble attracting attention—and holding on to it. Rapping can be traced back to the island of Jamaica, where it is called "toasting," a popular tradition at countless street parties where toasters grab a microphone and entertain partiers by improvising humorous spoken wordplays over a recorded beat. In Kingston, where toasting was popular at least as far back as the 1960s, rival toasters would try to outdo each other with clever insults and superior rhymes. These toasting battles became almost an institution. The audience's cheers would decide the winner. Toasting was brought to the United States by a Jamaican teenager named Clive Campbell, who immigrated with his parents from Kingston to the Bronx in 1967. By the mid-1970s Campbell had adopted the name DJ Kool Herc, and his south Bronx block parties quickly became famous. Toasters became known as rappers, or emcees, for master of ceremonies. And Herc provided another important innovation: When he couldn't afford to hire a live band he did the next best thing—he carried his turntable and loudspeakers out to the park and plugged them in. There was no extension cord long enough to run up to his apartment, so he broke open a lightpole stand and got his power there. He played vinyl records he already had lying around the house and he used his fingers to extend and repeat passages as they played on the turntable, especially the "breaks" where the singing stopped and the beat continued. By connecting different breaks from different records, he found, he could recompose songs in his own way, building up tension and juxtaposing sounds that might never be expected to go together. And the whole world of records, an entire universe of sound, was his palette. Sometimes he talked over the breaks in a rhythmic singsong to whip up the party, delivering shoutouts to friends who acknowledged their recognition by throwing a fist in the air.

Rapping was born.

If you look around today's hip hop world, you'll see that its most visible figures are all rappers: Eminem, Jay-Z, Snoop Dogg, Nelly, Eve, and Nas, to name but a few. There are exceptions, like the West Coast producer

Dr. Dre, of course, or multihyphenate producer, executive, and rapper Sean "P. Diddy" Combs. But it is the rappers who capture the public's attention. They command the microphone, spit the rhymes, and embody the swagger and style that gives the music its zing. They are hip hop's scowling face.

But it wasn't always that way. In the early years dj's ruled the spotlight. Before it occurred to any record executive to get it down on vinyl, hip hop was a live music form. And at the street parties that swirled for hours around the music, the dj was the hub of the wheel: the dj manned the turntables, chose the beats, and kept the party going. Dj's were once the people who played records for radio stations but the new dj's were musicians themselves, and on the street they were considered stars.

So it was no coincidence that hip hop's first big names were all dj's: Grandmaster Flash, DJ Kool Herc, Afrika Bambaataa, Davy D, and, of course, Jam Master Jay. Early hip hop dj's shared some roots with disco dj's. When hip hop was still struggling to its feet, a disco scene was in full swing at New York City nightclubs, and hip hop dj's surely borrowed some of their early ideas from disco jocks. Some of the more adventurous clubs, like Danceteria and Paradise Garage, served both hip hop and disco fans, and there was cross-pollination between the two cultures.

Hip hop was not born in Hollis but it took some of its first big steps there. Jason was thirteen in 1978 when hip hop first swept through his neighborhood. The attraction for him wasn't a fascination with rapping or scratching but rather becoming part of the fast-moving scene that was developing around it. Years later he remembered that no one imagined that this new thing called hip hop would ever make a dollar, let alone become an industry. "I was a drummer and I played guitar," he reminisced in an interview with the magazine *DJ Times*. "At the time that was the hottest thing to do. Then I just moved into being a DJ when that turned into the hottest thing." For the teenagers of Hollis hip hop was merely another fad, just like disco or funk music—that happened to be within the reach of anyone. "Back then it was all a hobby," remembers Hurricane. "Something to get us off the street. We never thought it would be a career."

But perhaps Jason sensed that there was something more behind this new culture. After attending a couple of the street parties that were popping up in the neighborhood parks, Jason quit the funk band he had been rehearsing with and plunged into deejaying. "Really it was just overall being part of the music that was firing me up," he recalled. "It was the overall vibe of the music, of the dj setting up the speakers, of the actual bringing the equipment out, being a part of the party, being the band. That was more of what inspired me."

Jason began practicing on his parents' turntable in the family living room, spinning records, cutting back and forth from the vinyl to the radio, synchronizing the beats, and pretending he was performing for a live audience. More than a few rock-and-roll generation parents banished their sons' and daughters' guitars and drums from the house, but Connie very quickly understood that Jason's hobby—despite the noise—kept him homebound for hours, and every hour spent hunched over the turntable was one hour not in the streets where trouble was always waiting. The following Christmas she gave him his first turntable, a Technics SL-10. An unused kitchen table was moved down to the basement and Jason now had a dj table. With a cheap Gemini brand mixer provided by a friend, Jason now had all the basic tools to be a dj, and over the weeks and months that followed he and his friends hardly ever left that basement. When they got tired they repaired upstairs to Jason's bedroom to record audiotapes of themselves. "I got to know that room well," remembers Garfield McDonald, who later served as technical director for Run-DMC. "The walls of Jay's room were covered in wood paneling that he had decorated with music and sports posters," Garfield recalls. "We'd sit around his room for hours talking about music and making tapes." Late at night when everyone else had gone home and the house was still, Jason fiddled with his equipment until he was so exhausted he couldn't raise his hands anymore. He'd catch a couple of hours of sleep, then get up and start again. "Waking up in your drawers is really a whole lot of fun," he told *DJ Times*. "Going to your set [equipment] with the headphones on in the middle of the night so that your parents don't know what you're doing when you're supposed to be asleep is great. I was rocking the bedroom." Jason decided to rename himself, adopting a catchy new handle—Jazzy Jase. Building a reputation as a dj would be far more difficult. Connie couldn't know it then, of course, but she had helped put Jason on the path to something special. At the same time, just a few blocks away, Joseph Simmons and Darryl McDaniels were spending hours making up rhymes in Darryl's family's basement on 197th Street.

There is true artistry in transforming a turntable into a musical instrument. Many people attempt to do it, but few can do it well. In the hands of a good dj, all types of music, from rock to disco to punk, salsa, pop, and even medieval chants, are merged seamlessly. The hip hop dj revolutionized music making by becoming the first artist to use records as the raw materials for creating new music. Like many great ideas, it was so powerful that it is amazing that no one had ever thought of it before. Hip hop dj's evolved two sets of formal skills: one, taking beats and rhythms by lifting them from vinyl records and turning them into something new. The second is scratching, the art of stopping and start-ing a record as it rotates under a phonographic needle, creating a blurry, percussive sound. The first dj to scratch was probably Grand Wizard Theodore, a thirteen-year-old Bronx wunderkind who started out as a protégé of Grandmaster Flash in the late 1970s. Those two skills, and the ability to blend sounds fluidly without interruption, formed the basis of deejaying. The hours and hours Jay put in manipulating his

turntable eventually began to pay off. Pretty soon he
was working with two turntables at once, the quantum
leap that put him into a higher orbit.

Jay was not the first dj to come out of Hollis. That
honor belonged to David Reeves, a Queens legend
who became known in Manhattan and the Bronx
under his stage name Davy DMX. He would later go
on to produce songs for Run-DMC, Kurtis Blow, and
countless other early hip hop acts. Jason usually liked
to say that his style was his own, but in a 2000 interview, when asked to name the dj's he learned from, he
said this: "I could say Davy D, Kurtis Blow's dj. He
was the one in the neighborhood doing his thing."
Jason watched closely, and he learned. "Jason was one
of the students of Grandmaster Flash and Afrika
Bambaataa and of course, Davy D," says his friend
AJ Scratch. "The only dj he ever gave props to was
Davy D."

"Jason used to come and watch me," remembers
Davy D, who still lives only a few blocks from where
Jason grew up. According to Davy D, Jason instantly
understood that there was an element of showmanship
involved, and grafted that onto his style from the start.
"I saw him grow as a dj and believe me, he grew fast. He
knew when to cut and when not to cut and he just knew
how to give a dynamic performance." During long
summer evenings in 1979, 1980, and 1981, Hollis lit up
on Fridays and Saturdays as hundreds of teenagers—
drawn by the new sound of dj's and rappers—began
congregating in the asphalt park next to Junior High

School 192. Located on Hollis Avenue and 205th Street, it is still known as "Two-Fifth Park."

On a Sunday in early December 2002, escorted by Jason's old friend Garfield, I walked around the outside of the tall cyclone fence that surrounds Two-Fifth Park. "Since Jay died the place is not the same anymore," Garfield told me, with melancholy muffling his already quiet voice. "Now people don't come out as much. There used to be benches and tables here. Jay would sit here and teach kids chess." He pointed to a barbershop on the far side of Hollis Avenue. "When Jay would come out of that barbershop he'd always stop on the street to say hi to people, and the next thing you know there'd be a crowd around him." The park gate was shackled and closed when we went there, but Garfield led me around to the east side of the park where we clambered through a large hole and stepped inside. Two-Fifth Park is about the size of half a football field, an uninterrupted stretch of asphalt with a basketball court along its north end. We walked to the southeastern corner of the park where Garfield suddenly stopped and gestured at the ground with both hands. "This is where we used to set up the deejay table." Two-Fifth Park is still remembered as a hallowed ground by the generation who hit their teen years in the late 1970s and early 1980s. The parties there were the prime social occasions of any given week, and a required event if you considered yourself cool. Hollisites talk about the park parties in the same reverential tone that

Grateful Dead fans once talked about Dead concerts: as
small utopias of great music and camaraderie, suffused
with the irreplaceable excitement of feeling as if you
were on the edge of something fantastical and new.
The street parties where Jason emerged as a dj have no
parallel today. There were no invitations—word of
mouth served just fine—and no schedule either. They
usually started around 8 P.M.—sometimes 9—and continued until 3 A.M. or 4 A.M. or until the police showed
up, whichever came first. These were the prototypes of
what later came to be called "outlaw" parties in many
different neighborhoods of New York, named that not
so much for the clientele they attracted, but for the
bold way in which they seized dull, ordinary public
space and transformed it into something special and
vibrant.

The park parties evolved a strict set of rules. Sometimes the dj would hand over the microphone to anyone who could muster up the nerve to step forward
and rap. Few were up to the challenge. The crowds
were exacting, ruthless judges, and anyone whose rapping skills were short of excellent could count on getting booed off in seconds. So the parties became
informal talent auditions, proving grounds for talent
and burial place for a lot of dreams. When two good
rappers were in the house at the same time, a rap battle
would decide who got control of the mike. Rap battles
were some of the most exciting moments of early hip
hop. One such battle is reproduced, Hollywood-style,
in the recent Eminem film *8 Mile*. Rap battles usually

began with one rapper mocking another, insulting his microphone skills and cracking wise on anything from his opponent's hairdo down to his choice of socks. The idea was to shout the other rapper down, but to do so with finesse and humor. Insults were required to ring true, or at least show great imagination, and cheap shots were frowned upon. Rappers took turns on the mike, after which the audience would decide who had prevailed, but usually a winner became clear before the end of the contest; audiences would hoot and laugh riotously when an insult found its mark. LL Cool J was a favorite battler and vanquished more opponents than anyone in the history of the park. It was survival of the illest: It took a razor-sharp wit and a lightning tongue to survive. In fact, rap battles have an intimate connection with the live traditions of blues and jazz. In 1958 the great novelist Ralph Ellison described live jazz in a way that seems to fit perfectly with the modern-day rap battles. "True jazz is an art of individual assertion within and against the group," Ellison wrote. It "springs from a contest in which each artist challenges all the rest; each solo flight of improvisation represents . . . a definition of his identity, as member of the collective and as a link in the chain of tradition."

Dj's engaged in battles, too, spinning back to back and inviting the audience to judge who could build the most exciting beat. Jay faced down dozens of challengers, rising to the occasion when he had to. One night he vanquished a challenger so badly that the challenger left the park in tears. The challenger had delivered a strong sequence that scored the approval of the crowd. But Jay followed and unleashed a flurry of scratching and stuttering beats that flowed so smoothly into a breakbeat that the crowd erupted in a frenzy that carried on for minutes. He finished off his opponent by crisscrossing his hands and hitting a few final, punctuating notes. The contest was over.

Jay wouldn't allow just any rapper to seize his microphone. A bad rapper might destroy the carefully tended flow of the party, a point of pride for him. Joseph and Darryl, who enjoyed rapping together, were among the few who were honored with Jason's mike. Run—nicknamed that because of his incessant chatter—had a natural flair with a microphone. Darryl, a bookish kid with large frame glasses, seemed more comfortable at home poring over his extensive comic book collection. But he had a way with words honed as a bright student in creative writing and English classes at Rice High School in Manhattan. "When we get our record deal you're gonna be our dj," he told Jason, as a way of thanking him for allowing him to get on the mike. But Darryl and Joe both hedged their bets: In 1982 Darryl enrolled as a freshman business major at St. John's University, and Joe entered LaGuardia Community College to study mortuary science. Joe figured he'd never go hungry in the mortuary business, but he daydreamed his way through his classes, and one day while looking at a cadaver he cooked up this rhyme: "One thing I know is that life is short/So listen up homeboy, give this a thought/The next time someone's teaching, why don't you get taught?/It's like that." Jason would later enroll at Queens College, mainly to keep his mom happy. "I was taking up computer science, but I really didn't want to be dealing with computers. I loved music. I was a dj," he told an interviewer.

For teenagers like Jason who were sixteen, seventeen, or eighteen and therefore too young to get into nightclubs or bars, these block parties were a wonderland of music and break dancing and excitement, not to mention beer and liquor and marijuana. "I was so young that they were the only way I could go out and have a good time," Jason once told a reporter. The parties were low-budget affairs done on the cheap all the way: Turntables and amplifiers were plugged into the base of the closest street lamp, which someone had to forcibly open and jerry-rig with a connection to a heavy-duty extension cord. The sound equipment was usually aging or decrepit. But these parties were still petri dishes of early hip hop, where dj's honed their skills, rappers vied for supremacy on the microphone, break dancers whirled and spun, and a new generation of young people became intensely aware of themselves and their new culture.

The earliest of these parties featured live bands. Before he started deejaying, Jason often pushed his way forward through the crowds, as close as he could get to the dj table so he could absorb as much of the technique of mixing and scratching as possible. "The dj was just between the bands in the beginning," he remembered, "the band would come on and everyone would run to the stage." As the night wore on, Jason became deeply enthralled by what was happening. He noticed that the party's most intense energy usually began flowing after midnight, when the band quit and the dj took over. "It was totally the dj and just the dj as the main attraction," he said to *DJ Times*. "The records he would play got a little better. And instead of closing [a song] and stopping, he would blend the records and keep it going. And he'd start talking on the microphone, asking the people to come party with him."

Darryl McDaniel, who showed up at many of these parties, explained to a reporter the allure for aspiring rappers like this: "You'd rap because you didn't want to be in a gang no more. You'd rap and join a break-dance team because instead of fighting you'd have break-dance battles." By the time Jason was sixteen he was well established with a reputation for delivering a great performance to all sorts of crowds. It's said that the most gifted dj's knew exactly where to drop the needle simply by reading the grooves in the vinyl. Jason was one of those who could hit a break right on the mark time after time. He became known for his exceptionally nimble fingers, an instant ability to read audience tastes, and encyclopedic knowledge of musicians and records. Jason schooled himself in the records that were forming the basis of the hip hop canon, such as the Incredible Bongo Band's version of "Apache," (which would become one of the most frequently copied beats of all time), Billy Squier's "The Big Beat," and Aerosmith's "Walk This Way." For months Two-Fifth Park was ruled by Jazzy Jase, and he had now accumulated a reputation as one of Hollis's best dj's.

The Two-Fifth Park parties eventually fell victim to their own success: Sometimes the crowds would build up to 500 people or more, which worried police. So, once the parties began spilling out into the streets and slowing down traffic, police began shutting them down. More often than not, though, the party would end by its own accord when a fight would erupt or some knucklehead would fire a shot, sending the crowd stampeding over the fences, and stopping the music dead in its tracks. Says Davy D: "I can tell you that more than once the party was going strong and somebody stupid fired a shot and the park emptied out faster than you could believe. Jason would be left standing there alone. He refused to just leave his equipment behind." It didn't matter. The next weekend the whole crew would come back and do it all over again. When Jason's parties got so popular that they outgrew Two-Fifth Park, the New York City Parks Department gave permission for the larger Jamaica Park to be used. For months the parties continued to flourish. Many a future star appeared and grabbed a mike: LL Cool J, the Fat Boys, and Salt-N-Pepa. Also mingling in the crowd was one Irv Lorenzo, who would later begin calling himself Irv Gotti, after the New York mafia don John Gotti, and become a highly successful record executive and head of his own record label, quaintly titled Murder Inc.

*　　*　　*

Jason was making money. It was a measure of his growing respect and clout in the neighborhood that one day
he rescued Run and DMC when no one would allow
them to get on the mike. No one, that is, not until Jay
showed up and said a few words. Instantly his friends
Run and D were given mikes and started rapping.

One of Jason's first paying gigs was at a Hollis bar
where a friend booked him to play weekends. The only
problem was that Jason was just fifteen years old and not
allowed in a bar. The owner's solution was to have Jason
dj in the back room, out of sight of most of the customers, and enter and exit through a back door. That
way he never set foot in the barroom. That turned into a
major gig for Jason, selling out both nights virtually
every weekend. Jason's haul was but a couple of hundred
dollars a night, but that was more money than he had before. With that cash he could keep up his equipment, buy
new vinyl whenever he needed, and pay someone to help
him haul his turntables around.

When Jason was sixteen he graduated to bigger gigs
and began throwing a weekly party at a Hollis nightclub called Dorian's. Admission was $3 for guys and $1
for girls. It, too, was an instant success. Jason was the
draw, and he spun records late into the night, watching
the crowds groove to his beats. The masses trying to
get into Dorian's often spilled out into the street.

Jazzy Jase was giving the city's best dj's a run for
their money. Hip hop was developing rapidly, and so
was Jason's career as a dj.

He was about to embark on the ride of his life.

four

BREAKTHROUGH

In January 1983 Jason threw a party at Dorian's for his friend Darnell Smith. Smith, as he was called, was a couple of years older than Jason, but the two had become good friends while Jason was still at Junior High 192. Smith was also a dj who performed under the name Nelly D. Together they made Friday and Saturday nights at Dorian's the party that kids traveled from all over the borough to get to.

That January night in 1983 Jason presided over the biggest party ever at Dorian's, which drew some 1,000 people and didn't wind down until 4 A.M. It was a gigantic smash hit. But as Jason walked home that night he was upset; his two favorite rappers and good friends, Run and DMC, were no-shows. That same night Russell Simmons had brought Run and DMC to the home recording studio in the attic of the producer and musician Larry Smith's house. Larry Smith was a few years older than Russell and was the most respected producer in Queens. He had already produced dozens of songs, including most of the work by Kurtis Blow, then one of the most famous rappers in New York City. Russell Simmons was Blow's manager.

The recording session took most of the night, but when the four men emerged into the daylight of the next morning, they had a demo tape that contained two songs: "It's like That" and "Sucker MC's." Run and DMC must have felt bad, too, because after a few hours' sleep, they went directly to Jason's house. "The next morning we talked and I'm mad at them," Jay told an interviewer. "But then they played the record for me and I was like, OK, I mean, I think they did the right thing."

Joe and Darryl had always promised that Jason would be part of the group if they ever got a deal and this was it. Jason was a little different from Run and DMC—more purely of the streets—but that was exactly what they were after. "He was a little rougher than us but I could see past all the hardness," Joe explained years later to VH1. That day, on the spot, Run-DMC became a trio. Jason was eighteen years old; Run and DMC were nearly nineteen. It was DMC who dreamed up Jason's new handle—"Jam Master Jay"—which had the same felicitous ring as Grandmaster Flash—and the new name instantly stuck.

In 1983 disco music was reaching creative exhaustion and a backlash was appearing on the streets of New

York City, Los Angeles, and London as legions of young music fans turned to the rebellious new sound of punk. Born in London's white urban underclass, punk held a powerful attraction for angry, alienated, working-class teens. It was positively ruthless in its disdain for authority and any sort of privilege, and its raw musical assault never missed a chance to remind you of the righteousness of its oppressed-class rage.

In many ways, hip hop presented a precise parallel to punk, only from an African-American perspective. As with punk, hip hop's raw, in-your-face rhythm and urgent rapping underscored a similar message: that the old, synthetic world of disco and funk music was collapsing and a new sound was here to blast away the debris. Rappers, like punkers, despised the phoniness of just about everything that came before them. For them, today was year zero, the beginning of a new history, and the slate was wiped clean. Rap music would not only entertain but also carry a message of clear, unvarnished truth. And music fans were clearly ready for something new, because both rap and punk accelerated rapidly through the 1980s. When punk began to stall around 1990, one of its offshoots, alternative rock, surged forward.

A few days after recording "It's Like That," Russell Simmons showed up with a copy of the demo at the offices of Profile Records, a tiny two-year-old independent label owned and run by two twenty-something executives, Cory Robbins and Steve Plotnicki. Housed in a small warren of offices in a high-rise building near 57th Street and Broadway in Manhattan, Profile consisted of the two executives and a staff of two employees. Profile had been launched with $34,000 the two owners had borrowed from their parents. But the label had not done terribly well in its two years of existence, and owed its survival to one of its few hits, "Genius Rap," by a rap duo calling themselves Dr. Jeckyll & Mr. Hyde. Profile, did, however, have something important working in their favor: They had an ear to the streets.

Robbins and Plotnicki had turned down other tapes Simmons had brought to them, but Simmons kept coming back. He didn't tell the Profile execs that none of the major record labels then had any interest in rap. "Profile was the best independent label at the time," Russell said in his 2002 autobiography, *Life and Def*, "which meant they might pay you a little bit instead of nothing at all." His persistence paid off because Robbins liked "It's Like That." "It was the first time I remember hearing a record with so few instruments," Robbins told me. "The whole approach was much more sparse." But he admits, he was not at all sure that it would be a hit. Two decades later the song is still remembered for its booming drumbeat, but it also offered concise political commentary written by DMC about the daily grind of life with not enough money and even less hope: "Unemployment at a record high. People coming, people going, people born to die. It's like that."

Profile signed Run and DMC to a contract. Jay

signed on as a full member immediately afterward, and the trio agreed to split their profits equally. Before turning the tape over to Profile, Russell wrote on its side label: "Run Dee-MC." The moniker stuck, but when Robbins asked Russell why the "Dee," instead of just "D," Russell shortened it to Run-DMC. DMC recalled in an interview with *SonicNet* that both he and Run thought that was a horrible idea. "At that time a name of a dj and MC group was like Grandmaster Flash and the Furious Five, and we wanted to be something good," said DMC. "Russell Simmons, Run's brother, called us and said the name of your group is going to be Run-DMC. It sounds so good now, but back then we thought it was the worst thing to ever come out of someone's mouth."

A few weeks later Robbins met Run and DMC and Jay for the first time. "They were eighteen years old and hadn't done much. They certainly didn't have much experience performing live. But at that point Jay was clearly an equal part of the group," says Robbins. Run-DMC is sometimes described as "the Beatles of hip hop." The comparison only goes so far, but Jason was in many ways like the Ringo Starr of Run-DMC. Both gave their groups its distinctive rhythms and both were late arrivals to the group—Jason missed out on the first recording sessions and Ringo joined after Pete Best left.

"It's Like That" hit the streets and seemed to fade. But six weeks later Profile discovered to its delight that it had a hit on its hands. In its first weeks the record sold about 500 copies a week, then 750. Around the sixth week they caught a break: A late-night weekend radio dj by the name of Mr. Magic at station WHBI started spinning it—usually sometime between 2 A.M. and 5 A.M. on his *Rap Attack* show. The results were spectacular. Sales immediately took off—first to 2,000 a week, then 5,000, and then 10,000. "It's Like That" and its B-side "Sucker MC's" went on to sell 250,000 copies and became the label's biggest hit ever. Profile was in the black, Run-DMC was in the green, and the record resounded throughout the world of music. *Rolling Stone* magazine later called it a groundbreaking record that marked the beginning of hard-core hip hop, and the death of the old R&B and funk-influenced style: "You can neatly divide rap history at Run-DMC's first single—'Sucker MC's,' " said the magazine. "It was as radical and influential a record as 'Anarchy in the UK.' " "Anarchy in the UK" is widely recognized as the record that launched and shaped the punk movement. "Before us there was no real meaning to a rapper," Jay once said. "Before Run-DMC came along rap music could have been a fad."

A second Run-DMC single—"Hard"—which was hustled into release—this time with Jam Master Jay on board—was aimed at catching the wave of excitement generated by the first single. It did well, too, selling 150,000 copies. It was the flip side of "Hard Times," however, that got the most attention. "Jam Master Jay," penned by DMC, announced to the world the identity of the man who was becoming the chief architect of the group's sound. For a few weeks in the summer of 1983 "Jam Master Jay" could be heard blasting from boom boxes and cool record stores all over the city. Its lyrics gave Jay a mystique:

> *J-A-Y are the letters of his name*
> *Cutting and scratching are the aspects of his game*
> *So check out the master as he cuts these jams*

"That song 'Jam Master Jay' made him sound like Elvis or something," dj Scott Hardkiss of New York City said to *DJ Times*. "Seeing them do it live and how a dj could rock a whole arena even blew my mind further." Dave Sirulnick, an MTV executive who got his feet wet promoting club concerts in the early 1980s, remembers the impact the song had on an energized and rapidly expanding hip hop audience. "Your dj was incredibly important back then. The dj was your band. He made you who you are, even more so than the MC. After the song 'Jam Master Jay' came out, something happened: it became very clear in everyone's mind that Jay was an equal part of the group. From the moment of 'Jam Master Jay' it was the three of them."

Jason from Hollis was suddenly catapulted into a higher orbit of recognition, and began gathering a cult of fans, just like Run and DMC. In the early 1980s giving a shout out to your dj was already an old hip hop tradition, harking back to clubs in the Bronx in the late 1970s. That tradition has long since faded: Today MC's rap about their producers, their record label, their bank accounts, their SUV's, even their jeweler, but rarely if ever about the dj. One reason is that with greater amounts of money and increasingly sophisticated production tools at their disposal, MC's no longer need to rely on dj's to the same extent that they once did. Now, prerecorded tapes, sequencers, and synthesizers do the same work, although purists would argue, with far less verve. When it came time for Run-DMC to record its first album, they made sure Jay was right there with them.

When Russell Simmons saw the numbers that "It's Like That" and "Hard Times" were putting up, he quickly began booking the group to perform anywhere he could. Although Jay had missed out on the group's first recording sessions, he immediately began rehearsing with Run and DMC to work out a routine for their live performances. In April Run was walking down a hallway at LaGuardia College when he heard "It's Like That" come on the radio. He created a small scene as he bounced off the walls shouting to passersby—"That's my song! That's my song!" Not long after, he dropped out of school so he could devote all his time to the group. DMC took a leave of absence from St. John's. "We were planning to go back to school in September but we got so hot overnight," Jason told a reporter. "I was amazed." Everyone was.

Run-DMC were soon hustling back and forth between Hollis and live dates in tiny clubs scattered across the city and New Jersey. Sometimes they performed two or three shows in a single night, each in a different borough, scrambling out the back door of a club in the Bronx to get to another club in Manhattan before some rowdy paying crowd vented their impatience on a poor concert booker. They usually were shuttled around in Larry Smith's blessedly spacious 1978 Cadillac, sleeping in the backseat whenever they could, except for Jay, who was too excited to do anything but listen to the radio and look out the window. Most of 1983 was a flurry of breakneck car rides and late-night performances at clubs, roller rinks, and warehouses such as Fantasia, the Foghouse, 371, Danceteria, the Audubon, the Roxy, the Ritz, Club Ones, and others. From 1982 to 1984, the Ritz on West 11th Street in Manhattan organized a once-a-week hip hop night, and Run-DMC was usually there to take the stage. For a moment, the Roxy became a home base for Run-DMC shows. Many years later, Jay had occasion to return there and joked about his familiarity with the place: "If you saw *Cats* on Broadway," he laughed, referring to the long-running production, "that was Run-DMC up here in the Roxy."

Some of these gigs paid them a few hundred dollars, others a thousand each, and some paid nothing at all. But the exposure created a fan base, and gave them sorely needed experience. "The first year Russell had us out there working for free," Jay told John Leland in *Spin* magazine in 1986. "That means a lot of towns had big packed shows, and Run-DMC was working free. He wasn't just trying to get money, he was trying to build something. So I love Russell for that, 'cause he built us." Russell was, as DMC once said, "almost like the fourth member of Run-DMC." It's not much of a stretch to say that it was primarily Russell's vision that raised Run-DMC from mere local fame to national fame.

Hip hop was still so new that on more than one occasion, Run-DMC arrived at a gig to set up and were greeted by a baffled concert promoter demanding to know where the band was. Jay later recounted how these exchanges usually went down: Promoter: "Where's the band?" Jay: "I'm the band." Promoter: "Where's the equipment?" Jay, pointing to turntable: "Right here." Promoter: "Then what am I paying for?" Occasionally a promoter would threaten to cut their fee, and Run would step in: "We'll never have a band. That's our band," he said, pointing to Jay. A lot of arguments broke out, but those became fewer when word got around of the high-caliber, crowd-pleasing shows they put on. Said Jay, "We ripped the crowd every night."

When a band works as much as Run-DMC did during late 1983 and early 1984, that band gets better, and by the middle of 1984 New York was buzzing about the excitement generated in live shows by the three young hip hop stars from Hollis. In those early shows the group established a format that never varied. Every live show started the same way, showing the confidence Run and D had in Jay to electrify any crowd. It was Jay, with a little help from Run, who dreamed up the group's signature opener. The first thing you noticed if you were a fan looking up and waiting for the show to start is that there were no instruments on stage: no drums, no guitars, just amplifiers, microphones, and, set upon a table, twin turntables. As the lights dimmed, the first figure to take the stage was Jam Master Jay, who took position behind his turntables and announced himself with a fusillade of scratching and thudding drumbeats that caused your sternum to vibrate a little. As the audience stirred, Jay teased them. "Are you ready to rock out there?" he screamed. Then louder: "I said are you ready to rock out there?" When the crowd answered back at sufficient volume, he shifted into a bouncing beat and called out: "What's my name?" The crowd roared back: "Jam Master Jay!" "What's my name?" "Jam Master Jay!"

Next he would begin scratching over the beat: "D! D! DMC! DMC!" As D hits the stage the sight of him triggers a frenzy. D raises his hand. "Are you ready for my man Run?" he asks, then adding in mock disappointment: "Jay, Run wants to come out here but this crowd ain't live enough. Lemme hear you! Y'all wanna see Run?" The crowd roars again. "Lemme hear you say Ruuuuuun!" As Jay scratches out "Run!" "Run!" a figure walks out of the darkness and seizes the microphone. The buildup is tremendous now and the crowd is screaming for release. Together on stage finally, Run, DMC, and Jay shout: "Run, DMC, and Jam Master Jay!"

Capitalizing on all the excitement, Run-DMC went into the studio in late 1983 to record its first album. Jam Master Jay was a big part of the studio team, contributing ideas and beats, and his scratching can be heard all over the record, establishing for everyone the sound of Run-DMC. In 1984 the group released the first album in rap history, simply titled *Run-DMC,* and it immediately took off. By the end of the year it had sold 500,000 copies. The album was not just a success for Run-DMC, it was a milestone for all of hip hop music, and announced to the world that the market for rap was potentially bottomless. Jay, Run, and DMC were given a $25,000 advance for the record, which they had to split with Russell and Larry Smith. They weren't rich, but, once again, it was more money than they had before. A video that accompanied the album, *Rock Box,* then scored the distinction of becoming the first rap video to be played on MTV, raising Run-DMC's profile enormously. It had another effect, too. While Run and DMC's faces were familiar to their fans, Jay's was not. *Rock Box* showed him in action, and for many viewers it was the first image they saw of a hip hop dj. Big jumps started coming quickly for Run-DMC. The clubs they played in got bigger, and the money got a little better. And getting added to MTV made them legitimate in the eyes of the pop world. You'd see a Police video, a Don Henley video, and then a Run-DMC video. They were in good company.

Mostly on the strength of Run-DMC sales, Profile turned into a hugely successful label and was for years the largest indie. Run-DMC followed their debut album with a second, *King of Rock,* that became the first hip hop album to sell 1 million, and eventually would go on to sell nearly 4 million. "They were in a way the whole company," says Robbins. "They built the label. Ninety percent of our sales were Run-DMC." At its peak, Profile had thirty employees. "People always said to me, you guys are doing great, but what if this rap thing goes away?" Robbins told me. "I can laugh at that now." Robbins sold out to his partner for a substantial sum in 1994, and in 1999 Profile sold its rap assets to Arista for a multimillion-dollar price tag.

Thumb through any photo history of hip hop and you'll be amazed at the ostentatious assortment of glittering pants and multihued jackets worn by rappers during the late 1970s and early 1980s. Look at the first wave of rap artists, at groups such as Soul Sonic Force, and you'll see yards and yards of getups that would not look out of place on Michael Jackson today, or perhaps on a magician in Las Vegas. Anything was possible, because the rules had not yet been written. The hip hop duo Dr. Jeckyll & Mr. Hyde actually performed in three-piece business suits and power ties, and are still believed to be the only rap group to ever do so. Most early rappers had no better ideas, so they rummaged through the closets of R&B and soul acts for inspiration until they came up with a look that they imagined said "hip hop." Their short reign of excess ended when Run-DMC appeared. They took their look right off the streets of Queens.

Run-DMC's style became the look that nearly all of hip hop would imitate. Its genius was in its boiled-down simplicity: white athletic shoes (Adidas preferably), black jeans, leather jackets, and black velour hats, sometimes but not always touched off by a thick gold neck chain. Run-DMC's wardrobe sent a message to anyone watching that clothing counts, but it also sent a second message: We're not going to let the clothes wear us. And that was a message that kids on the streets could get down with. Asked about the group's wardrobe, DMC explained in a 1998 interview that it was a key component of their success: "We didn't have no costumes, we came dressed as is, and that's what made the fans relate to us more than any other rap bands because when they looked up on stage and saw us it was like looking in a mirror." What DMC didn't explain was where their look came from, and the answer to that is it came from Jay. Jay was always the most stylish of the trio, and he had settled on his look very early on.

In one of the earliest photos ever of the three, probably snapped in 1982, Run and DMC still look like goofy high school students with their baggy clothes and turtlenecks. But Jay looks like a budding musician. His oversized belt buckle spells out his first name. He is clad in a sleek black leather jacket and black hat. It was the Run-DMC look, alright, in the making.

One day at a rehearsal, Russell Simmons took one look at Jay's outfit and ordered Run and DMC to dress like that. "How I dressed in high school is the way we dress now," Jay later explained to a reporter. "The black hat, that's mine," he said. "The Adidas, that's me. My

vibe is our vibe." And where did Jay develop his look?
"Jay had 'hood in him that Run and DMC didn't," dj
Ed Lover told me. "When he was a kid Jay was hanging
out up on Hollis Avenue with the thug dudes and the
dice cats. He wanted to look like them."

The only place Jay bought clothes was on the Avenue,
the place immortalized in the Run-DMC song of the
same name. The Avenue is an open-air gallery of shops
lining both sides of 165th Street in Queens, with the
street made into a broad walkway. Closed off to cars, it
is the center of action on weekend afternoons.

A few weeks after Jay passed I went to the Avenue to
have a look. The Avenue draws everyone from teenagers to pensioners, and a steady stream of shoppers
flowed past. I spotted more than a few young hip hop
fans still sporting the Run-DMC look, the leather jackets, the black hats.

The Avenue is mostly crammed with discount stores
now, places where you can get a wig or discount jewelry, leather jackets, sheepskins, bomber jackets, or
Jay's favorite, black Lee jeans. Jay's favorite store, Mr.
Lee's, is gone now. But for a dozen years it was where
he purchased his Adidas, his jeans, and the fur-lined
overcoats known as "snorkel" jackets. The footwear
was always shell-toe Adidas, partly for comfort, but
mainly for style. The shell-toe held its crisp white look
the longest, and rested comfortably on the foot even
without laces. That, too, was a Jay innovation. Jay liked
to match his shoelaces with the rest of his wardrobe.

One day when he got tired of changing laces he went out without any laces.

Another style was born.

Although their look was carefully chosen to send a message that they come from the streets—not from an album cover—the clothes created the effect of having been casually selected. It was a marketing masterstroke that goes back to Jay, and dovetailed perfectly with Run-DMC's authentic, unadorned street sound. For fashion-conscious high school kids eagerly looking for new trends but vigilantly guarding against anything that carried a whiff of marketing, this was the perfect answer. And it allowed Jay and Run and DMC to be themselves, not gussied-up entertainers.

MTV's Dave Sirulnick remembers that "Run-DMC's look was so stripped down that it turned attention back on their rapping. What was important was what they were saying." Russell Simmons recognized more than a little bit of irony in the fact that it took three middle-class kids from Queens to find the street look that resonated so sharply with hip hop fans. In his autobiography *Life and Def,* Simmons commented: "I've always thought it takes a bit of a suburbanite—as we were, coming from Queens—to see the power in ghetto culture."

There was one fashion trend that DMC inadvertently launched on his own. One day he turned up at Run's house wearing eyeglasses, but not just any glasses, the large-framed, slightly squared-off brand known as Gazelles. They were magnificently geeky. In fact they were so extremely geeky that they came out on the other side and became strangely cool. Run told DMC to wear them every day. He did and soon an image was born. Although DMC retired the glasses recently in favor of contact lenses, the Gazelles were imitated all over Queens.

The beats, the wardrobe: It was no exaggeration to say that much of the juice powering Run-DMC's main creative circuits came from Jam Master Jay. "Jay was really the backbone of Run-DMC," says dj Ed Lover. "The group's whole style came from Jay, in more ways than one."

It's a long way to go from the corner park to the front door of a record label. And it's even farther to scale the record charts, but in 1983 and 1984 Jay had achieved them all. The path to success in hip hop had been blazed: conquering the parks, conquering the clubs, making hit records, and then conquering arenas.

There was only one of those left for Jay to do.

five

WE THREE KINGS

Now he's the Jam Master, and we're the MCs
Like lightning and thunder, we're knocking down trees.
—Run-DMC on "Jam Master Jammin' "

Like many great groups, Run-DMC's division of labor allowed the talents of each of its three members to mesh perfectly. Run was the group's charismatic face and natural-born loudmouth who once quipped to an L.A. radio jockey about the dedication of his fan base: "When I talk, like E.F. Hutton, they listen." D was the behind-the-scenes lyricist, rhyme maker, and bottomless well of cheeky couplets such as "You can't touch me with a ten foot pole/I even made the Devil sell me his soul."

Jay was the beat master—the heart of the group, and in many ways the keeper of the flame. It's difficult to overstate the importance of the dj to the early days of hip hop. All of the music was made without instruments, so the dj was responsible for spinning every inch of the sonic backdrop against which rappers would leap off into their verbal flights of fancy. The entire performance—sometimes an hour or longer—

rested on his shoulders. "Jam Master Jay made no mistakes," says Chuck D, the former rapper of the great '80s and '90s rap group Public Enemy. "He set the pulse rate of the whole group and he moved from beat to beat seamlessly. I heard him spin many, many times and there were never any cracks in his wall of sound."

The producer Larry Smith remembers that "Jay took the dj job very seriously. He listened to records over and over again and took them apart with his ear. He was so precise and knew what every part was. He could look at the grooves in the vinyl and know where exactly the break was. He could drop the needle right in the groove exactly where he needed to be every time." At a club gig in Charlotte, North Carolina in 1984— one of Jay's very first as a member of Run-DMC— Smith recalls that they drove most of the day to get there and everyone was exhausted but Jay, who was buzzing with nervous energy and couldn't wait to get on stage. "He set up his equipment well before anybody else was ready and he carried his bag of extra needles with him all the time, like he was guarding a bankroll. Those needles were important to him in case one of his turntables messed up."

Those unfamiliar with Run-DMC often imagined Jay, who seldom rapped, to be a silent partner of sorts who kept behind the turntables while Run and DMC roamed the stage. Run and DMC are credited with originating the art of cross-talk in rap, that is, alternating their rapping within a line, and weaving and doubling up their voices to create a shouting, attention-grabbing effect. But in a way Jay spoke more loudly than them all. Of all the signature sounds the group developed over the years, Jay's rhythmic fireworks are likely to be remembered the longest. Run-DMC's beats—which are Jay's beats—permanently changed the sound of hip hop. With his in-your-face sonic assault and raw, muscular rhythms, Jay captured the pent-up energy of the streets and reflected it back on his audience. He loved volume—the more the better—and was fascinated by all the things he could do with a good drumbeat. To a generation of directionless Reagan-era teenagers, the thunder of his mixing and scratching was positively electrifying. There was something visceral and thrilling about the act of him making music with his bare hands, without an instrument in sight, as if this were a new art form being born before their eyes.

Watching Jay on the turntables was to witness an impossibly fast stream of musical ideas pop into his head and get instantly flashed to his fingertips where they would take form. With his hands criss-crossing and headphones pressed against one ear, he punctuated his notes by throwing his mouth agape, or twitching his head to the rhythm. Jay was a perfectly respectable dancer, too, twirling and rocking behind his tables with panache.

Run-DMC's extensive early touring spread the gospel of hip hop around the country. From a standing start—from scratch, you might say—in the early 1980s it swept out of New York and rapidly engaged urban teenagers everywhere—in Philadelphia, Los Angeles, Houston, Miami, and Oakland. Those kids were all soon marching to the beat of hip hop. The revolution that had been launched in the Bronx a few years earlier was now being redirected by Run-DMC—and the path ran right through Jam Master Jay's turntable. Hip hop's first wave of artists, including Grandmaster Flash, Whodini, the Sugarhill Gang, and a handful of others who scored the music's first hits, quickly found themselves losing traction when Run-DMC came along. Their softer, R&B-influenced style of rap seemed artificial and showbizzy next to Run-DMC's austere presentation of big beats and high decibels. Run-DMC's stripped-down music sank its roots deeply into the pavement of tough African-American neighborhoods everywhere. In doing so Jay and Run and DMC created a new sonic language that virtually all future hip hop groups would have to follow. Among its rules: that hip hop is above all about realism, and realism starts in the street. Second: that hip hop's voice comes with an explicitly political purpose—to puncture the everyday hypocrisies floated by authority figures. And third: the message of the music is to prick the conscience of society and to help the world feel the hopeless condition of poor and underclass youth.

From the very start, Run-DMC's music intertwined these messages with rousing beats and clever wordplay. The range of subjects they addressed was unlimited: from big things like unemployment and loneliness in the crowded city to quotidian matters such as what type of beer to buy or the best footwear. In 1984 J.D. Considine of the *Washington Post* wrote that "even their most outrageous rhymes are delivered with such undeniable flair that it's hard not to take them at face value." *Rolling Stone* magazine noted that under the influence of Run-DMC rap adopted a new tone and experienced a rejuvenated commercial life: "Rap music, which had seemingly peaked in popularity, suddenly rebounded." Soon culture critics joined music critics in appraising Run-DMC's power.

Writing in New York City's *Village Voice* in April 1985, Greg Tate described the group as "literate and thought-provoking," and he marveled at its ability to mix exciting rhythms and provocative writing that enabled them "to crack incisively on white and black culture alike without missing a beat." Tate optimistically concluded that "hip hop can become more the cure of the condition of black underclass youth than a symptom of it."

Although Run was the front man, the group functioned like a democracy, with three free-floating but interdependent parts. Run had a knack for plucking clever song ideas from the small daily experiences he had—in the park, on the subway, daydreaming on the couch, or as in the song "You Be Illin'," waiting in line at a Kentucky Fried Chicken. DMC could improvise in an instant, reeling off strings of rhymes with ease, such as "The name's McDaniel's not McDonald's/The rhymes are Darryl's, the burgers are Ronald's."

Jay once described their songwriting process this way: "Run comes up with the initial idea. Dee writes mostly the rest of the record. . . . Then I'll come up with the music to it. I'll arrange it and then we put it all together. Nobody has the formula. We all have it." That is exactly how one of their bigger hits, "Peter Piper" (from the *Raising Hell* album) came together. Using his drum synthesizer and turntable, Jay composed a beat he liked and, as he explains, "I scratched and Run and DMC said a couple of rhymes. We would rhyme and stop, rhyme and stop. They said the first thing and then I scratched on top of it."

Jay would spend hours and hours with his headphones on, experimenting with various techniques of mixing and scratching and blending beats. When asked to explain the process, though, he made no claim to any particular genius and instead revealed his method as simple trial and error. "You take what you've got in your head and go put it down. If it don't work, do something else," he said. "That's how it always works for me." Since hip hop existed only in a very basic form before him, he was essentially self-taught. "Jay worked very hard at it," says Larry Smith. "That's all he did for a long time—practice."

Jay didn't mind putting in endless hours because the process of discovery was so exciting. Hip hop's flexibility and lack of well-defined borders meant that its sources were potentially infinite, and his inspiration could come from anywhere, and often the unlikelier the better. Sometimes he grabbed snippets he heard on the radio and spliced them into songs. Other times it might be a passage off an old Temptations 45-rpm single. The only thing they had in common was they appealed to Jay's omnivorous musical appetite—and in his words, as long as they rocked.

"It's just the feel for sure," Jay told the entertainment magazine *BAM* in 1986. "I might be turning a radio for my normal hip hop station and I'll run across a record that the drummer is just playing and I can't believe it sounds so good." And Jay was an extremely observant student who carefully studied what else was out there and absorbed it. "I remember whenever we'd go to a new city he always liked to go to clubs or parties after the show," Smith continues, "not to just hang out, but to hear what other people played, so he could know what was hot. I'd go with him sometime and he would just sit there for hours and watch and listen." To borrow a phrase once said by a famous jazz trombonist about a fellow musician, "His ears are like a vacuum cleaner."

The comfort Jay felt wandering into strange clubs in strange towns stemmed from his experiences coming up on the streets of Hollis. It didn't get much tougher than that anywhere, and he had not only survived, he had made the streets work for him. He carried himself with the kind of self-possessed confidence that veterans of tough neighborhoods get, a mix of triumph and cool. The street that once posed so many risks and consumed so many of his friends had been tamed, and he had made it his tool. He was not afraid of anything.

Years later, Jay would say: "Always, I'm always on the street. Whenever there's some hip hop going on, I'm in the house."

Of course, hip hop was very different then. Gangsta rap had yet to be born, Tupac Shakur and Biggie Smalls were still unheard of, and the music put a premium on humorous verbal dexterity and skillful scratching. "Jay motivated Run-DMC to be Run-DMC," says AJ Scratch, a talented dj who befriended Jay in the early 1980s and remained close to him over the next decade and a half. "With a turntable he created a new world. There was more deejaying back then and less everything else. No samples, no tapes, you had to put it down by yourself. Now hip hop is about money and bling bling, but back then it was really about the dj. People wanted to know, What can you do?" DMC boiled things down in a 1999 interview with Philadelphia's *City Paper*. "We do that artform that was born before 'rap' was made," he said: "playing records live and boasting and toasting, no glitter, no playback, in basement parties and parks."

Reviewers often singled out Jay for praise. One critic writing in the New York newspaper *Newsday* spoke of him as more than simply a dj: "Jay's mastery of the twin turntables has developed to the point where his scratch mixes stand as coherent, complete songs in their own right, rather than mere sonic collages."

In a 1986 review of *Raising Hell*, *Rolling Stone* wrote that "DJ Jam Master Jay works the turntables like a

brain surgeon turned mad scientist. This is one group
that defiantly 'don't need no band.' " The reviewer
went on: "Jay lays down a classic hip hop mix of beats,
bells, scratches, squeals, and static while the MCs apply
their twisted tongues." A year earlier the magazine was
just as enthusiastic in its review of *The King of Rock.*
"When you add ripped up drum tracks, Jam Master
Jay's scratching and cutting, and the percussive vocal
interjections of Messieurs Run and DMC, you've got
the most comprehensive attack in rap." The hip hop
monthly *The Source,* catching Run-DMC at New York's
Radio City Music Hall in 1993, reported that "deejay
Jam Master Jay orchestrates matters with breathtaking
authority." 1986 brought Run-DMC a rather considerable honor: They made the cover of *Rolling Stone* magazine, the first hip hop group to do so. From 1983 to
1988 they enjoyed one of the more remarkable runs in
pop music history, rising from Hollis basement parties
to million-selling records, arena tours, and international recognition on Live Aid.

For Jay it was a ride that he never wanted to end.

In the world of the dj, you're only as good as the music
in your crate, and Jay knew his way around his crate
better than anybody. Says Chuck D, "He was the most
knowledgeable dj out there at the time. He knew who
did what record, what label it was on, who the artist
was, and what the musical component was that he
could use." Good dj's all have a little archaeologist in
them. Discovering a rare or out-of-print record is the

dj equivalent of finding a sacred scroll. Jay built his collection by scouring old record stores on the Avenue and in Times Square in Manhattan. One of his regular stops was Downstairs Records, a grungy but fabulously well-stocked store that is probably familiar to anyone who ever passed through the 42nd Street and 6th Avenue subway arcade during the 1970s, 1980s, or 1990s. (Downstairs later moved to an upstairs location on Sixth Avenue.) Dj's adored Downstairs for its row upon row of obscure and hard-to-find vinyl, a vast treasure trove of tens of thousands of 12-inch, 33's, and 45's that spanned soul, R&B, Latin, Caribbean, rock, metal, and virtually anything else you could imagine. And long after compact discs began taking shelf space away from vinyl, Downstairs Records remained true to its roots and its specialized clientele. The store's bright fluorescent lights and incessantly blaring music beckoned curious passersby and party-bound dj's hunting for something fresh late into the evening. Jay also spent lots of time in record shops located on the Avenue—where he could pay as little as 25 cents for a 12-inch, or as much as $50 for a rare, vintage album. The dexterity and musical knowledge he built up studying vinyl and wandering in obscure record shops whenever he was on the road made him more than ready for the task when it came time to go back into the studio.

Almost every big music group follows a familiar arc: Wild, exciting days and nights on tour turn into the musical equivalent of forced labor as the fun wears off and the group yearns to escape the revolving door and claustrophobic existence of hotel rooms, arenas, stage-door exits, and midnight room service. Yet most learn life in the studio can be a grind of equal proportions, just with less space. The Beatles staged only two U.S. tours in their entire career but they still broke up spectacularly in 1970. Why? It was the forced intimacy of the studio—not Yoko Ono—that eventually caused their personal peeves and simmering resentments over money to irretrievably boil over.

"We are lifelong friends," Jay told a writer in 1987. "We are closer than anyone can imagine. Run-DMC is more than a band. It's more like a unit, a bond. We have everything in common." That was something of an exaggeration. The group seldom socialized outside of work. But when they were together the bonds were very strong and very real.

When music observers today look back and wonder how the three members of Run-DMC weathered seven albums together over eighteen years, people close to the band often credit Jay. In the studio, Run was known to get testy occasionally, as was DMC. When disagreements sparked, Jay was usually the one to calm inflamed emotions. Former Profile Records exec Cory Robbins remembers Jay as a steadying ballast in the group, even from their very first days. "Run and D were crazy in their own way," Robbins says. "When Run is in the mood, he would talk nonstop. No one else in the room gets a chance to say a word. D was very quiet so you never knew what he was thinking. But Jay was always normal and sensible and consistent. If there was some problem, he was the one you could go to." Whenever Run and DMC got angry at each other and stopped speaking, Jay acted as the conciliator, talking them both down from their anger.

John King, owner of the studio where Run-DMC did most of their recording, remembers Jay as "a rock. When things weren't going right he was the one you'd talk to. He was efficient and he always had his act together. He was the guy who really held Run-DMC together." Chungking Studios was a charmingly cramped hole-in-the-wall of a recording facility located on the sixth floor of 241 Centre Street on the edge of Manhattan's Chinatown. It has since relocated to a more spacious, better-equipped, and rather elegantly appointed penthouse location across town on Varick Street. When you exit the elevator into Chungking on the twelfth floor, you find yourself hemmed in by two heavy-duty glass doors that are secured with electronic locks. A security camera keeps watch. To get from the outer lobby into the studio waiting area you have to be buzzed in by a receptionist. No one gets in Chungking without permission. Once inside, you notice the vaulted ceilings and gold and platinum records adorning just about every inch of its walls. Chungking is owned and run by King, an eccentric former rock musician and producer with salt-and-pepper hair and live-wire energy. The studio became a recording Mecca for hip hop acts in the '80s and '90s, and was an occasional haunt of Tupac Shakur. The studio became so popular among rappers that at one point King emptied the soda machine and restocked it with Olde English 800, the brew of choice among many old-school rappers.

King's studio began getting business from hip hop acts after he had a chance meeting with Russell Simmons and Rick Rubin at the club Danceteria in the early 1980s. The studio later gave birth to a large percentage of hip hop's greatest hits, including LL Cool J's *Radio*, and the Beastie Boys' *License to Ill*. From 1984 until 1999, it was the house studio for Def Jam Acts and virtually the entire Run-DMC catalog was recorded there. The name Chungking started life as sort of a joke, a piece of doggerel that popped out of the mouth of producer and Def Jam Records co-founder Rick Rubin one night. It was also a play on King's name and the studio's Chinatown location, and it stuck. King's original name for the studio, Secret Society Records, was lost forever.

Run was never one short on ego to complement his prodigious talent. "Run was the Mick Jagger and the Axl Rose of the group," says MTV executive Dave Sirulnick. In Run's autobiography, *It's Like That*, he modestly describes himself as "the raunchy, dynamic, microphone-throwing Michael Jordan of hip hop." That sort of hubris may be a compensation for growing up as the youngest of three brothers and having to fight for everything he got. His entrance into hip hop was thorny. His first job was papering neighborhoods with concert flyers announcing upcoming rap shows.

Then things picked up for him. His next job was as a dj performing with Kurtis Blow, who was then being managed by Run's older brother Russell. "I know my brother and Kurt were having a great time," Run told *Rolling Stone* in 1986. "I wanted to be with them." But even though Run had been dreaming of becoming a rapper since he was twelve, Russell was slow to warm to his brother's microphone skills. He was forced to live in Russell's shadow, as Russell became first a celebrated manager and producer, then record label owner. All the while he built up a competitive streak that still remains in him. Perhaps because he always felt he had to prove something, Run grew into an exceptionally forceful presence on the microphone, with a booming shout that could rouse the dead.

DMC, sometimes called the quiet member of the group, seemed to live two lives, almost like the ego and the alter-ego of one of the comic book characters that he loved so much. When he was young he spent most of his time over pen and paper, reproducing the superheroes he saw in his comic books. Part of his obsession with comics may have come from the fact that for years his strict, no-nonsense mother Bannah, a nurse, did not permit him to hang out in the parks. While his friends were out drinking beer and smoking marijuana and listening to music, DMC was stuck in the house. He began rhyming by himself in his attic, too shy to do it in front of anyone else. Alone upstairs, he created new personalities for himself; as he told writer Bill Adler in *Tougher Than Leather*, they carried names like Easy D and Grandmaster Get High. Then one day his parents gave him enough money to buy two turntables and a mixer. He and Run set up their equipment in Run's basement, a space they called their "laboratory," and spent as much time as they could practicing their skills. DMC told Bill Adler that he learned that "rapping was more fun than being a deejay for me cause I could get on the mike and tell people how devastating I am."

After jazz music, hip hop music became America's second great original art form. Although there are plenty of social critics and politicians who do not concede the "art" part of that equation, they need only look at the music that is thriving beneath the purview of the popular press. They'll find that hip hop's conscience and humanity and highly skilled wordplay and musicianship do exist in a variety of places: in the thought-provoking songs of the Brooklyn rapper Talib Kweli, in the uplift and social conscience of the Chicago rapper Common, or in the acute political critiques of Oakland's Michael Franti and Philadelphia's the Roots.

By the early 1990s rap was a gigantic industry and before 2000 arrived it would be well along in its crossover into the cultural and commercial mainstream. Baggy pants, athletic jerseys, unlaced sneakers, even the styles of speech coined by rappers were picked up and copied by kids of all economic classes and all races. By 1998 some 80 percent of the hip hop records sold in the United States were bought by whites. Barely four years later hip hop sales would tally a staggering $5 billion and help the record industry to strong profits when genres such as alternative rock and R&B were slowing down.

Overseas there was the fascinating new development of dj culture. In Manchester and London, England, dj's were experimenting much in the way hip hop dj's had years earlier and they were adapting their music to commercial formats that were gaining stature. In the middle 1990s dj culture produced bona fide stars such as the American Moby whose fame lifted off from his soundtrack to the motion picture *The Beach,* and Brits like Fatboy Slim and Paul Oakenfold, who started his career as a European talent scout for Run-DMC's label, Profile Records. In the United States Funkmaster Flex, DJ Premier, and DJ Clue counted themselves as students of Jay's.

In one way or another all of them stood on the shoulders of Jam Master Jay. He took the turntable where no one had ever taken it before.

Jay's influence gave hip hop a solid foundation on which to build, and even can be said to have made possible the style of L.A.'s gangsta rappers. It's hard to imagine Dr. Dre's *The Chronic* in 1994 without there first being a Jam Master Jay. *The Chronic* made a giant breakthrough for hip hop music by linking 1970s funk with 1990s hardcore rap. When you see Dre today he is almost a direct extension of the style Jay set down more than a decade before: firmly rooted in the 'hood and exacting in its awareness of style. Where Jay wore leather and Adidas,

Dre is almost always clad in athletic wear of some kind, fresh white sneakers, perhaps a basketball jersey, and usually jeans. There is nothing fancy or excessive. The almost monkish purity hip hoppers harbor, requiring that everything that touches them have a stamp of authenticity, comes directly from Jay.

He didn't know it then of course, but looking back now, Jay symbolized an era of comparative innocence in hip hop, an era that took delight in the simple pleasures of rapping and scratching just for the fun of it. It's not being curmudgeonly or uncool to say that much of that early energy has disappeared from hip hop music today. And hip hop was lucky to have such a marquis personality as its representative.

Some performers wear fame like an ill-fitting jacket; it hems them in, restricts them, and forces them to try to live up to an image that they imagine the public expects.

Jay wore fame well. It suited him perfectly.

six

IT'S A WONDERFUL LIFE

There's a lovely photo taken in the summer of 2001 of Jay, his wife Terri, and their three boys, Jason, Terry, and Jesse Trey, all smiling and smartly turned-out in white formal wear. The picture captures one of those moments that every happy family experiences, when everything feels right and the future looks safe and inviting. The occasion was Jay and Terri's tenth wedding anniversary. That day was also a chance for the couple to do something they had wanted to do for years but could never quite find the time: celebrate their marriage in a big way.

Jay and Terri had married in a resort in the Poconos on June 24, 1991 with just a handful of family and closest friends present. A few days later they held a larger ceremony at a church in Manhattan for about thirty people. By 2001 Jay's career was sailing forward, he had a little money in his pocket, and the time was right. So to make their tenth anniversary memorable, Jay chartered a three-decker 150-foot private yacht. It turned into a memorable night indeed. Even the weather cooperated. The rain that had been falling all day tapered off, and as some 250 guests—all dressed in white, too—streamed onto the boat on that late-summer afternoon, the sky cleared. A red carpet was rolled out along one of the upper decks and as the families and a large group of friends looked on, Terri, in a bridal veil and wedding dress, walked down the aisle. In front of a gigantic display of flowers, she and Jay reaffirmed their vows. Jay's best man, his old friend Randy Allen, said some words and then the Rev. Bernard Jordan blessed the couple. Lastly, Run stood up and gave them a heartfelt tribute. As the yacht slipped away from the Manhattan shoreline and floated south down the Hudson River, the guests listened to music and chowed down on a five-course menu that included shrimp, crab, and unlimited champagne.

The night was magical. When the boat rounded the lower tip of Manhattan and pointed its nose eastbound momentarily, the passengers could see off the port side of the boat the Brooklyn Bridge and beyond it the Queensborough Bridge uptown in the distance, and the lights of Queens Boulevard stretching east toward Hollis. As they turned back south with lower Manhattan at their backs, Jay and Terri soon got a great close-up view of the Statue of Liberty, which was spectacularly lit up that night. A few minutes later they passed underneath the twinkling beacons of the giant

Verrazano Narrows Bridge, which spans Brooklyn with Staten Island and marks the entrance to New York harbor. Not too long after, talking about all his personal riches, Jay told VH1: "I got my wife, I got my kids, I got my health, I'm so happy to be here, that everything is always OK with me." Jay and Terri kissed and danced late into the night.

Terri was Jay's second serious relationship. In 1984 Jay met and began dating a Queens woman named Lee, and they instantly hit it off. They moved in together, first living in the basement of Jay's mother's house. With some money he had earned as a dj, Jay had the basement remodeled, making it comfortable for the two of them. He brought in a refrigerator, a bed, installed a bathroom, and put up a wall so they'd have a little privacy. He also bought a couple of color tvs— one for his mom and one for himself—a vcr, and a little gold jewelry to wear around his neck.

In 1985 Lee gave birth to a baby boy, and they named him after his father. When the young family outgrew his mom's basement they moved into a house just down the block that Jay rented. Jay's father's death three years earlier had forced Jay to change his attitude about life, but now he had a baby boy to support, and he took the responsibility seriously. His relationship with Lee would not last—they decided to split soon after Jason's birth—but they remained close and shared custody, and Jay vowed to be a presence in his son's life, and he was. He made a regular habit of taking Jason with him for jaunts around Hollis and whenever he went on the road, he always returned with a gift for his son. Jay was but twenty-one years old and already separated, with a new baby to support and a career to nurture. But as the door closed on one relationship, another one opened.

Jay used to tell his friends that he fell in love with Terri the moment he saw her. It's not difficult to see why. It was more than her obvious beauty. Great beauty can be distancing. Sometimes it carries with it a hint of arrogance. But Terri Corley Mizell has both a strikingly beautiful appearance and a warm, reassuring manner that puts people at ease. Their first meeting was by pure luck. Jay had just landed in New York on a break from touring when he spotted her in an airport. He decided to strike up a conversation with her. It went well and he came away with her phone number. That was extraordinary in itself and a tribute to Jay's charms and polish as a conversationalist because the young woman he approached that day is as no-nonsense as they come. Terri hails from a very strict, conservative family who sent her to Catholic schools in Manhattan, demanded good grades, clean diction, and elegant attire at all times, and taught her to carry herself with an upright self-confidence. Her mother hails from Puerto Rico, her father is African-American, and she grew up bicultural, learning to love Latin music and cooking as well as American radio stations and hamburgers. She speaks fluent Spanish and English and prefers jeans, sneakers, and a leather jacket to high heels.

Terri's mother and father separated when they were young and she and her younger sister Camille were raised primarily by their maternal grandmother, Asteria Torres, in the Amsterdam Houses, a public housing project on the west side of Manhattan. The Amsterdam Houses sit within sight of the Metropolitan Opera House and the ballet theater of Lincoln Center, which happens to be the original setting of the romantic Broadway musical *West Side Story*. Terri, her sister, and her mother all worked at one time or another as airline flight attendants. Terri resigned shortly after the 9-11 attacks on the World Trade Center and the Pentagon. She was five years younger than Jay, and still in her teens when they met, so her grandmother forbade her to date. For the first couple of years of their relationship Jay was not allowed to visit their apartment, so he would ring the bell and wait for her to come downstairs. A good part of their courting took place in the courtyards of the Amsterdam Houses and strolling the streets of the Upper West Side. Jay often changed his schedule to be with her. Terri was too young to be admitted to nightclubs, so they found other entertainment. One of their very first outings was a double date to a Chinese restaurant in Soho with his friend Hurricane and Hurricane's new girlfriend Dawn. Hurricane and Dawn met the same day as Jay and Terri. (Hurricane and Dawn married in 1990. Jay was their best man.) When Terri turned twenty-one, she and Jay married. Guests at the Manhattan reception say the music switched between Puerto Rican salsa and American hip hop, and everyone danced enthusiastically to both, including Jay's mother, Connie. Many of Jay's Hollis friends arrived in hip hop formal wear: fresh white Adidas and black hats. The party wasn't big but it sure was noisy. Jay and Terri quickly built their own family: Their two sons came along in 1992 and 1995.

Many young men in the record industry, particularly those with money in their pocket and the burnish of celebrity, enjoy a long bachelorhood. It's no secret that the record industry attracts an inordinately high number of exceptionally beautiful women, many of them attracted to the same things that the industry's men are: the glamour, the money, and the nonstop excitement of concerts, dinners, and exclusive parties. The fast-lane life offered by the record business is a tempting perk, but Jay seemed to realize that its pleasures were transient and false. He never devoted much time toward pursuing fashion models or actresses or the other sorts of trophies that go to the industry's stars. Nor was he one who felt a need to make the scene every night, to show his face at exclusive parties and preen for cameras. His idea of an exciting night was a few hours in the studio, maybe a dinner somewhere with some friends, then perhaps hooking up with a couple of Hollis guys for a drink and a couple of hours of music in a club.

In 1988, about two years or so after he started seeing Terri, Jay packed up his musical equipment, some clothes, said good-bye to his mom, and moved to Manhattan. It was a big move: It was his first time living away from Hollis and he was excited about being near the center of the action—the clubs and restaurants and the center of the city's music scene. The early '80s was a wonderful time to live in New York. Artistically, the city was fertile and alive. Downtown music clubs like the famed CBGB's hummed to the sounds of what came to be called the "art rock" scene, groups like the Talking Heads, Suzanne Vega, and Sonic Youth, who hung out in galleries with painters and at theaters with filmmakers and made challenging, perceptive music. Alternative rock was still in its youth, and bands like R.E.M. were building their reputation by giving shows wherever they could. The Police, the band led by Sting, were breaking big, and Madonna, then a young singer trying to make it, was still hanging out at Manhattan nightclubs. And of course, hip hop was young and robust. New clubs were popping up everywhere around town and on any given night there were hundreds of possibilities. For Jay, more accustomed to the limited options of Queens, this was an eye-opening experience, and he plunged into his new life.

Jay rented a loft apartment at 111 Barrow Street in Greenwich Village and turned it into his bachelor's pad. He had new wall-to-wall carpeting installed—all black of course—and outfitted the place with luxurious leather couches and chairs. Those were black, too. To break up the monochrome, he bought a new dining room set and end tables done in green and trimmed in black lacquer. 111 Barrow was the site of some legendary parties that reeled out until 4 or 5 A.M. And Jay's place became a crash pad for anyone from Hollis passing through the city and in need of a place to stay. In fact, there was rarely a week when there was not some old friend sleeping on the couch for a few days, or some pal hanging out for a while to help Jay with this project or that project.

There was also an opportunity for Jay to indulge himself a little. He bought himself some new wheels—a Mercedes in his favorite color. He loved to fill the car with friends and go for rides around the city. If the outside temperature fell below 70 degrees, Jay eagerly demonstrated to anyone who happened to be with him that his car had the latest in creature comfort—heated seats. Jay had only two requirements in cars: They had to be big and they had to be black. One of his first purchases was a Jeep Wrangler. Next he bought a Lincoln-Continental, then the black Mercedes, which he followed with a minivan, a Toyota Land Cruiser SUV, and finally a Lincoln Navigator, one of the biggest trucks on the road. That was his favorite, because he could ride seven passengers in it if he needed, and still have a little room left over for his equipment.

If you spend enough time reminiscing with Jay's close friends, you start to hear stories about his generosity. At first as I heard them, I thought these stories were embellishments, fond recollections from faithful friends grown bigger with each telling. Then I began to hear the same story told by different people in Jay's life. As I looked deeper, I found that they are all true. Jay enjoyed the money he earned, but he seemed to get even greater pleasure by spreading it around. When the first of his Run-DMC checks began coming in, he went on a shopping spree and bought his mother a car. Over the years he bought cars for lots of people—one for his sister Bonita, one for Garfield: "He tapped me on the arm one day and handed me these keys," Garfield says, still smiling at the memory. He pointed Garfield out the front door. Parked on the street was a shiny 1985 black Cadillac. "I got in and drove it home right away," Garfield told me, "before he had a chance to change his mind. That was my first Cadillac."

On another occasion, after Garfield admired one of Jay's thick gold necklaces, Jay showed up a couple of days later with a bag in his hand. Without saying anything, he tossed the bag into Garfield's lap. Inside was exactly the sort of gold "rope" he had admired. Jewelers I spoke to say that much gold can cost about $5,000 or more. Davy D tells a story that shortly after he and Jay had agreed to produce some records together, he mentioned in passing that he had never ever had $10,000 in his bank account at once. Jay laughed and said, "Oh yeah? Well, watch this." Jay and Davy worked together for several months, after which Davy got his $10,000, which he used to buy his first Mercedes. Over the years Jay probably purchased three or four cars for his mom alone, at least one for his sister Bonita, and one for his brother Marvin, and who knows how many others for his close friends.

A night out on the town with Jay was always an event to be remembered. He loved to show up at a nightclub or at the backstage door of a concert with two dozen friends in tow. Some musicians have entourages whose job it is mainly to stroke the star's ego, look cool, and run up the tab. There seems to be an inverse relationship at work: the more inflated a star's perception of himself, the larger the entourage. But when Jay appeared with two dozen people following in his wake, you could bet that they were all friends, not hangers-on. His personal guest list at Run-DMC concerts usually ran as high as thirty people, and occasionally when concert organizers balked at allowing so many people in for free, Jay told them to just take it out of his paycheck.

Jay was never one to pull star tactics. But if the doorman still refused, he'd let him know that they could either allow his friends in the door or find someone else to dj that night. Inevitably, every door swung wide open for Jay and his gang.

In nightclubs he often couldn't resist picking up the bar bill for everybody in his party. His friend Orville Hall recalls Jay dropping $2,000 to $3,000 some nights on bottles of expensive champagne that he spread around among his pals, even if his wallet might have been temporarily running on empty. "If Jay was drinking that night, you were drinking, too," says Hall. Jay would roam the bar and make sure everybody had a glass in his hand. The routine got so familiar that often a crowd of people would follow him from place to place and wait for him to buy drinks. "I saw him spend a lot of money on people he hardly knew," says Hall, "but that was Jay." If there was ever a strange face in the crowd, Jay usually took a minute and chatted. It was important to him that everybody felt like they were part of his group. "Anybody who was starstruck by him would have lost that in ninety seconds," says Jim Tremayne, editor of *DJ Times*, who ran across Jay many times at professional dj events around the world. "He was very comfortable with his status as a star dj and that resonated with people when they were around him. People felt relaxed around him, never like they were in the presence of a big star. The funny thing was though, he was a big, big star. He just never carried himself that way."

If Jay couldn't buy something, he figured other ways to extend himself. His pal Kool E tells a story of getting caught short one night at a lounge he owned on Jamaica Avenue when the dj he had hired to spin was unexpectedly a no-show. Kool E had a club full of people and no one on the turntable, surely a prescription for a bad night. His luck changed when Jay just happened to drop in for a drink. "Jay stayed there all night spinning for me, using my old turntable and a cd player. He did it all night, and by all night I mean until 4:30 A.M. He kept the party going for me. All I did was make sure he had anything he wanted to drink. Nobody ever knew who it was who was spinning, and Jay never charged me a cent. That's the kind of people Jay was."

On that anniversary night, when it came time for the

boat to turn back, the party was still going so strong they ordered the captain to keep the boat in the waters another couple of hours and add it to their bill. As the party swung into the early morning, Jay probably couldn't help but feel a little amazement and pride at how far he'd come. Hardly six years ago he was still spinning records in his mother's basement. Now he was throwing a party that was costing $25,000—and he could probably afford it. The party was full of VIP's, including Russell Simmons and Lyor Cohen, but Jay also made sure that his unfamous friends were in the house, too—Big D, Kool E, Hurricane, Davy D, all the Hollis guys who were with him at the beginning. The all-inclusive touch was very much Jay—honoring his roots and affirming the value of the pals who were there when there wasn't any money. It was the kind of gesture that is uncommon among stars of his stature. The record business is notoriously filled with opportunists and fair-weather friends who cling to success like lint on a pair of nice pants. And it's not unusual for successful artists, when surrounded by these new friends and advisers, to sever their ties with their past. It's a way of reinventing and repackaging themselves as they'd like to be seen, not how they are.

Sometimes it's an image thing: It wouldn't look good, say, for record-buying fans to discover that a fearsome stage presence like Marilyn Manson, rock's prince of darkness, was once a pimply music journalist in Florida who—gasp—dressed in regular men's clothing. If a little reinvention is called for, many musicians won't hesitate. More than a few rappers have rewritten their personal history to accentuate the tough-guy persona they project on records, telling journalists highly exaggerated tales of gunslinging, drug dealing, or other criminal bravado. It makes good copy. But the trouble with that is sometimes someone from an artist's past can unexpectedly step forward with memories that don't match the rewritten version.

Christopher Wallace, the late rapper better known as Biggie Smalls, learned that the hard way. Before he was killed in a drive-by shooting in Los Angeles in 1997, Biggie built a massive following and a rep in the rap world as a former drug dealer. His hair-raising exploits as an entrepreneur on the streets of Brooklyn gave his wonderful rhyming an undeniable realism. He was forced to enter the crack trade, he once explained in song, because times were so hard that he had nothing to eat. Biggie suffered an embarrassment when his mother, Voletta Wallace, who raised him as a hardworking single mother, happened to mention to a journalist that there was always food on the table in the Wallace household, contrary to Biggie's claim.

Jam Master Jay never got caught in such fibs because he never tried to reinvent himself or leave his past behind. In fact, he always brought it with him. Jay's assistants, his security people, his roadies, technical advisers, and most of his producers all hailed from Hollis. In an interview with *Melody Maker* magazine Jay expressed a nugget of wisdom that some music stars never quite get. "You must be respected at your home," he said, referring to the old neighborhood. "That's the people we *need* respect from. They're the people we grew up with. They love you for just being you." His bigger bank account, his cars, that was all great for a kid from Hollis, but he made it clear that the money didn't make him, he made the money. "Money doesn't change us," he told a reporter from *Rock Fever*. "Nothing changes us. We're still the same people." And it was true.

Jay spent most of that night on the boat in summer 2001 catching up with old friends, retelling the old war stories from their childhood, and laughing uproariously. Jay loved more than anything to reminisce, and his memory for detail made him an excellent raconteur. As the boat finally made its way back to the Hudson River pier where their voyage began, Jay was at the center of a knot of old friends animatedly talking. "Jay loved to remind you exactly how something happened, and how he felt at the time, and why it was so funny," says Hall. "It was a big part of friendship for him, to remember the old stories and let you know exactly how much he valued those old days. It was cool to be able to still be with the same people he started off with. That really meant something to him."

Davy D was one of the last off the boat that night and walked with Jay and Terri back to their parked cars. "He was really excited that night," Davy remembers.

Jay and Terri could have lived anywhere they desired— Manhattan, suburban New Jersey, but they decided to settle back in Queens. They chose a spacious new house with picture windows and a handsome burnished-wood face, and plenty of room inside for the kids and Jay's extensive music equipment. The house sits on a hillside just a few minutes' drive from Hollis on a block of neat brick homes with European cars parked in the driveways. There is a coach light in Jay and Terri's walkway, leading across a well-kept lawn that is bracketed by professionally landscaped bushes. Two wooden deck chairs sit on a small terrace, and hanging near the front door is a wooden plaque that reads "Welcome." Jay bought Terri a sleek black Lexus sedan, which she zipped around in, picking up the kids and running errands. Staying in the old neighborhood does not by itself make you a better person, or automatically worthy of admiration. Nor does leaving it. Many who leave the 'hood quickly demonstrate that the 'hood never left them. Is there anything more annoying than the sight of a famous, privileged athlete or musician who earns millions of dollars a year and lives in a mansion but still winds up in tangles with police, and cannot properly contract a verb on national tv? For all the millions of words and gallons of ink that have been spilled romanticizing the raffish allure of street life, the 'hood is in reality a difficult place, and sometimes a dangerous one.

Choosing to return to Queens, as Jay did after he married, would have been meaningless if he had put himself in a large house behind a fence and tried to live in the neighborhood while remaining separate from it. But he was not making a political statement or nurturing his image—he was coming back to something reassuring and friendly and familiar. It was the place he felt the safest, and the most at home.

Even in the late 1980s and very early 1990s when Run-DMC was riding high as the most famous rap group in the world, Jay continued to be an accessible presence in Hollis. Anyone could reach him. All you had to do was open up the Queens white pages. His home phone number was listed there. To the merchants along Hollis Avenue he was still a regular face dropping in to buy sodas and chips on Saturday afternoon, just like he had when he was a schoolkid, only now he usually had one of his sons with him. And even in a barbershop full of customers, everyone listened respectfully when he spoke.

Every Fourth of July Jay would return home to Hollis, to his mom's old house, and throw a big block party out in the street. The Fourth of July party was a tradition going back a decade or more. Even if Jay was on tour somewhere, he always took a break, hopped a plane, and would show up at his mom's house just as things were getting underway. Garfield usually deejayed at these affairs, and the party was open to anyone who happened to come by. All the old faces would come out: Larry Smith, Davy D, Hurricane, Runny Ray.

By the time darkness fell 203rd Street was usually packed with party-goers, and somewhere in the mass was Jay, savoring the warmth of being at home again. Jay loved fireworks and each year he made a point of stocking up on them before the party. He traditionally capped off the evening by sitting back in a lawn chair and firing them up into the sky over Hollis.

When the night was done, Jay often had to catch a plane out the next morning to rejoin the tour or get himself to a dj date somewhere.

Then, with his battery recharged from a visit home, he was ready to take on the world.

seven

ON THE ROAD

Before he became a dj, Jay seldom ever ventured beyond Hollis, but as Run-DMC's popularity multiplied in the mid-1980s, the group began receiving invitations to play all over the United States. Soon invitations were pouring in from Europe and Asia, too. Hip hop's growth during those years was breathtaking. From its meager commercial beginnings on 12-inch records and in grungy nightclubs it became, in just a few years, a globe-crossing phenomenon, selling out arenas and large concert halls. For the first time since the British rock invasion of the 1960s that brought the Beatles and the Rolling Stones to America, and the punk attack of the 1970s that delivered the Sex Pistols and the Clash, the musical tide was flowing in reverse.

In 1985 Jay and Run and DMC made their first trip abroad—a ten-day tour through England where they performed four shows, two in London, and one each in

Manchester and Nottingham, to appreciative but somewhat baffled audiences for whom hip hop was new. Over the next few years they would travel even more widely: to Tokyo, Kobe, and Nagoya, Japan; to London, Paris, and Amsterdam; to Switzerland, Finland, and Sweden; and to Germany, Poland, the Ukraine, and Australia.

Jay loved the road. It was relief from the closeness of Hollis and an escape from the relentless hustle of New York City. He saw the Eiffel Tower and rode the Metro around Paris, which he found amazingly quiet and clean, and nothing like the subways at home. He was stunned to see that one of the Parisian Metro stops even had paintings hanging on its walls that no one defaced. On a trip to Munich Jay and Run and DMC were met by representatives of Adidas thrilled at the publicity Run-DMC was giving their athletic shoes. Three Mercedes-Benz sedans—one for each group member—were purring outside on the curb, waiting to ferry them to their hotel. For the entire stay, whenever they went out to sightsee or to grab something to eat, the fleet of Mercedes awaited them. Every day on the road was some kind of new adventure. One night they performed at a club that was draped in Adidas banners. The next day as they sat in a restaurant picking over their food the actress Drew Barrymore suddenly came over to their table. She was in Germany making a picture called *Babes in Toyland* and happened to be staying nearby. "Are you guys Run-DMC?" she asked. "You are! I think you guys are so cool, you're my favorite band!" Run and D were not so sure who *she* was, but Jay told them she was the star of the movie *ET.*

When they got to London, Jay and Run and DMC were so excited that they ran their luggage carts through the airport as if they were competing in a bumper car race. When they learned that they had been booked in a Holiday Inn, Jay, a connoisseur of hotel rooms, put the kibosh on that and they called ahead from the car and found a nicer place in London's West End.

Jay loved London. He enjoyed London's Piccadilly Circus because it reminded him of Times Square, and he was so impressed by the sheer size of Buckingham Palace that he made a point of returning to it whenever he came back to the city. Something about London's landmarks agreed with him: perhaps because they were all things he had read about as a kid at Junior High School 192 in Hollis. He loved seeing Big Ben and Trafalgar Square and he couldn't leave without at least once getting on a double-decker bus. And he always stopped at a gift shop somewhere to pick up something for the family. He looked forward to the group's rides between cities. They were long periods of downtime— a rare commodity for him in those busy days—and he cherished the chance to kick back and think. He always brought a pair of headphones and a tape deck with him on the tour bus, and as they rolled through the European countryside he spent hours listening to tapes and enjoying the scenery.

For kids from the insular world of Hollis, this was a dazzling new world indeed.

But mostly Jay relished being turned loose in a foreign city, free to explore the record stores and nightclubs and late-night scenes. Even after a long day of interviews, photo ops, a concert performance, and a group dinner, he was usually the last one back to the hotel at night. Jay was intensely curious about seeing and meeting local people wherever he went. The British press loved him. In London one night he collared a reporter for *Blues and Soul* magazine who had been sent to interview the group and insisted on a tour of the city's hot spots. So while Run and DMC went back to the hotel, the obliging reporter took Jay to a weekly dance party at a nightclub on Charing Cross Road called Buzby's. Buzby's was a hot scene then, full of some of London's coolest characters, and a few of them recognized Jay right off, although it probably was not hard in his white shoes, all black attire, and black hat. He was soon caught up in conversation with a cluster of curious partiers fascinated by his clothing and eager to know what life was like in "Hollis." They seemed disappointed when he told them it wasn't so different from many other cities.

Some of the kids knew the words to Run-DMC's songs. At one point a young woman recited to him the words to "Jam Master Jay"—she had them perfectly memorized—and when she finished the two of them broke out laughing and Jay congratulated her. For the first time he got a sense of the true power of his music. Here he was, 3,000 miles from home in a foreign land, and he runs across a fan who knows his music almost as well as he does. Jay drank British beer—surprised that it was served lukewarm, of course—and listened to the dj spinning cuts for the crowd. And he watched the kids dance in herky-jerky movements that were entirely different from anything he had ever seen at home.

His nightcrawl was not yet over. Big Ben had already struck midnight when he and his nightlife tour guide caught a ride and carried on to a jazz club called Wag, where Jay loved the scene. American late-night clubs were inevitably smoky and packed with young people. This one was relaxed and low key and full of serious jazz fans who kept a hush throughout the set and savored every note that was played. Jay was tickled by the clothes the English wore, and he was particularly enamored of the British accents and how sophisticated they made everyone sound. It was about 4 A.M. when Jay finally got back to the hotel, but it had all been worth it. The British press gave Run-DMC high marks, and several of its critics focused on the manner in which Jay juxtaposed different sounds: "Run-DMC's simplicity has always been a masterpiece of unconscious compression, where things that didn't go together were crammed into one unit, so close that they seemed to have belonged to each other forever," wrote a critic in *Melody Maker*.

One thing Jay never quite adapted to, though, was foreign food. Even in France, home to some of the world's best cuisine, Jay would often beat a path to the nearest McDonald's and fill up on hamburgers, just in

After the funeral, Terri comforts her sons Terry and Jesse as they leave the cathedral. *AP/Wide World Photos*

Inside the flower-filled cathedral packed with mourners, Reverend Run and DMC gave Jay a heartfelt send-off. "Jay was not a thug," said DMC. Added Run: "Let's not ask why Jason is gone. Ask why we are here. Jason helped build hip hop, and his work is done." *AP/Wide World Photos*

ABOVE: The Hollis Crew, clad in the outfits made famous by Jay—velour hats, leather jackets, and fresh white Adidas—carry Jay's casket into the church on November 5, 2002. *AP/Wide World Photos*

BELOW: At the 1988 Grammy Awards, Run, DMC, and Jay basked in the spotlight and enjoyed the moment as they became the first hip hop act ever to receive a nomination for a Grammy. *AP/Wide World Photos*

Rapper Chuck D (center) was among the crowd that quickly assembled outside Jay's studio on the night of October 30. *AP/Wide World Photos*

View of rear exit of Studio 24/7 in Hollis, Queens. Jam Master Jay's body was brought down this fire escape stairwell by New York City morgue workers late on the night of October 30, 2002. *David E. Thigpen*

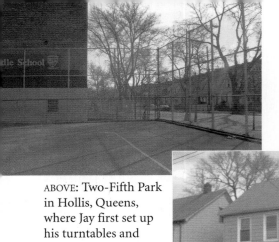

ABOVE: Two-Fifth Park in Hollis, Queens, where Jay first set up his turntables and drew hundreds of teens to his weekend hip hop parties. Lightpole on right side is where he plugged in his equipment. *David E. Thigpen*

ABOVE: Jason Mizell's childhood home in Hollis, Queens. *David E. Thigpen*

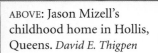

LEFT: Front entrance to Studio 24/7 on Merrick Boulevard where Jam Master Jay was shot and killed on October 30, 2002. *David E. Thigpen*

RIGHT: In the beginning: Sometime in 1984, copping a squat on a bench in Two-Fifth Park, where Jay first built a rep as the best dj in Queens.
Glen E. Friedman

BELOW: Jay, on right, shows DMC and Run the art of cool as the three take a minute to chill out back in Hollis in 1988.
Glen E. Friedman

Jay had a natural flair for theatrics and grew into hip hop's most excitingly watchable dj. This hands-crisscrossed move was one of his trademarks, and drove the crowds wild. *Glen E. Friedman*

In 1986, when the song "My Adidas" became a smash hit around the country, Adidas awarded Jay with a solid-gold Adidas sneaker to hang on his neck chain. Sharing the moment are Hurricane (left, in black hat) and Grand Master D (in tan outfit). *Glen E. Friedman*

LEFT: In 1985 Jay was sporting the look that would become the signature style of hip hop: black Lee jeans, black leather jacket, black velour hat, and a cooler-than-cool expression. *Glen E. Friedman*

BELOW: At the Manhattan nightclub the Ritz, where Run-DMC often performed in the mid-1980s, Jay punctuates a beat by throwing his hand in the air. *Glen E. Friedman*

Street kings: Run and DMC and Jay captured in a light moment on the sidewalks of Hollis in 1985, just before they unleashed their act on the world. *Glen E. Friedman*

On top of the World: After the success of *King of Rock* and *Raising Hell*, Jay treated himself and bought this fully decked-out Jeep. Unfortunately, it was wrecked on Christmas night 1987. *Glen E. Friedman* case the menu at that night's restaurant or banquet did not agree with him. After arriving in Paris one night Run-DMC were welcomed to a lavish hotel reception and dinner in their honor prepared by the hotel's chef. But the dinner went south when the first course arrived—which happened to be a seafood salad with fish—the whole fish, that is, head and all. The next day Jay went to a market and bought a supply of bread and cold cuts that he kept in his hotel room refrigerator for emergencies.

But nothing could top their arrival in Tokyo. Run-DMC had come to Tokyo as part of one of the final legs of the *Raising Hell* tour. They had been on the road most of that summer, so Jay and Run and DMC were tired, anxious to get home and escape the life of airplanes and hotel rooms. The flight to Tokyo had taken a full day. What they would see in Japan, however, would make the long journey worthwhile. As they came off the plane, bleary-eyed from the interminable flight, they spotted a crowd of young people waiting for them. Fans frequently awaited them in many cities they went to, so this was nothing new, but as they looked closer they couldn't believe their eyes. There waiting for them in the terminal were hundreds of Japanese hip hop fans, sporting black fedoras and white Adidas with no laces. Some of them stood with their arms folded over their chests, a pose Jay had made famous in old press photos and music videos. Other fans sported gold neck ropes and Kangol hats.

The fans clustered around their heroes with worshipful smiles, snapping photos and extending posters for them to autograph. The cluster of kids—about 100 of them—followed them through the airport causing quite a scene. When Jay and Run and DMC got to their hotel, there were hundreds more fans waiting, sporting Run-DMC t-shirts and warm-up suits and gold chains. Tokyo, to their shock, had developed a vibrant hip hop scene. Although few of the fans spoke English, that didn't stop them from knowing the words to every Run-DMC song they had ever heard. As Jay got out of his car to enter the hotel some of the kids began chanting the words: "He's Jam Master Jay the big beat blaster/He gets better cause he knows he has to." "We didn't expect that at all," Jay told the magazine *Rock Fever*. "That was the furthest thing from our mind coming to Tokyo. Kids at the hotel. They were waiting on us."

When the group arrived in Nagoya and Kobe, there were similar scenes outside their hotel. Amazingly, some of the fans had their hair cut short a la Run-DMC, and a few of them looked as if they had stayed too long underneath a sunlamp. There were culture clashes, too, for sure. When Jay left the interpreter behind one day and hopped into a cab to go sightseeing, he couldn't understand why the cabbie kept getting so angry at him. Then he realized he had been slamming the door shut every time he got in and out. Those Tokyo cabs had automatic doors. Run-DMC performed over three nights at arenas that held about 3,000 fans and made a smash hit.

Run-DMC's tour of Switzerland was a success, too,

but among the group members it will probably be best remembered for the epic food fight that broke out in a Swiss hotel room between Run-DMC and the Beastie Boys versus a corps of international music photographers. Later on, in another light moment, Run-DMC and the Beastie Boys were lined up for a photo op and Jay or someone in the group pushed one of the Beasties just as the shutter snapped. As each one in the line falls into the next, the picture captured what resembled a row of laughing dominos as they all toppled over into the next.

In Australia, enthusiastic fans trailed Run-DMC wherever they went, and one presented DMC with what he later admitted was the coolest gift he had ever received from a fan. It was a stuffed Koala Bear wearing gold chains, Adidas, and a black hat. Unfortunately DMC inadvertently left it in the luggage bin on the long plane ride home. When he realized he had left it behind he phoned the airlines, but it was gone.

In Amsterdam Jay and Hurricane and DMC one day went in to investigate one of the city's famous smoke shops, sampling some of the product when someone spotted a plate full of chocolate chip cookies. Jay and Hurricane helped themselves. The cookies tasted great, so they ate more before DMC saw what they were doing and stopped them: "Do you know what those are? Those are space cookies. Magic cookies. You're gonna be stoned for two days!" Jay and Hurricane went back to their hotel and slept it off.

*   *   *

The catalyst for hip hop's worldwide expansion was Run-DMC. Their sound was becoming bigger, their razor-edged rapping even sharper, and their live work was winning them converts everywhere they went.

In the summers of 1984 and 1985 hip hop's first big U.S. tour hit the road under the name Fresh Fest. Fresh Fest was a huge financial gamble. Although there was clearly a sizable market for hip hop music, no one had ever been crazy enough to put up the money to string together a series of concert dates, simply because no one knew just how dedicated those fans were. A concert promoter by the name of Ricky Walker was the one who finally took the risk, booking concert space in thirty-five different markets and contracting with just about every rap act available. Many of those acts were barely established at the time. Walker was an unrecognized logistical genius who successfully harnessed the many artists involved while judiciously balancing the scores of competing egos, a superhuman feat considering that he had to run a hellish gauntlet of obstinate managers and selfish record labels to get there.

He hired Run-DMC to headline the tour for a fee of $5,000 per night. Each night they capped off the show. Wearing their black fedoras, black Lee jeans, and unlaced Adidas sneakers, Run-DMC made an unforgettable impression on thousands of teenagers who became instant rap fans. Making sure that everything went smoothly for Run-DMC was their road manager Lyor Cohen. Jay was so impressed at Lyor's management style that he later suggested to Russell Simmons that Lyor ought to be promoted. Lyor was promoted a few times, and is now CEO of Island Def Jam Record company.

Jay had no idea if the tour would last two dates or ten, but he was thrilled to be getting his feet wet in the big-time concert business and eager to try out some of his moves in front of a large crowd. "He wasn't nervous," remembers Hurricane, who attended many of the tour dates in the Run-DMC entourage. "Jay was performing in front of crowds since he was five. So this was the same, just a little bigger." Jay quickly honed his showmanship. Whenever he scratched out the opener of "Jam Master Jay" the crowds erupted in a frenzy. So he learned to put in a moment of silence—just one or two beats' worth—after launching into a hard-rocking rhythm, to ratchet up the tension and playfully extend the audience's anticipation. Then he would engulf them in sound.

He was also becoming fluent in deploying all kinds of counterpoints and catchy sound effects: cowbells, bass notes, cymbal crashes, and car horns. He was a flurry of motion at the dj table, headphones draped around his neck, each hand manipulating a turntable. "That tour established Jay," says the producer Larry Smith. "All those high-profile appearances made him the most famous dj in the country. He was it."

Rick Rubin remembers that "the scale of Jay's personality really came through in a big setting. He held the audience's attention. He was the focal point. A lot of DJs never caught your attention, but Jay brought charisma to it as a performer."

Fresh Fest is now remembered nostalgically by hip hop fans for its wonderful lineup of the Fat Boys, Whodini, LL Cool J, and Run-DMC, but at the time it was plagued by uneven quality and inconsistent sound systems. Of course, any conspicuous failure such as fan violence or a poor turnout would have almost certainly scared off skittish future promoters, setting hip hop back years. Somehow though, the first Fresh Fest managed to make about $3.5 million, and like that, the hip hop tour was born. Fresh Fest confirmed what many believed but never could prove: that hip hop was here to stay, with a solid retail base to prove it. The next summer Fresh Fest 2 hit fifty-five cities; once again Run-DMC was the headliner, and this time it pulled in even more money—about $7 million.

On July 13, 1985 Run-DMC took a one-day break from Fresh Fest and caught a plane from Savannah, Georgia to Philadelphia to perform at Live Aid, the giant worldwide benefit concert cooked up by Irish rock musician Bob Geldof. Run-DMC had never faced more than 10,000 people before and now suddenly found themselves before what would be their largest audience ever—some 90,000 fans assembled at JFK Stadium in Philadelphia—and a worldwide tv audience of hundreds of millions. Live Aid was held simultaneously at Wembley Stadium in London. Although their performance was left out of the MTV broadcast, Run-DMC held their own, performing between Ozzy Osbourne and Rick Springfield, in a show that featured the likes of Madonna, the Police, and Tina Turner.

After a string of success, Run-DMC was ready for bigger things.

In the spring of 1986, a few months after Run-DMC released their third album, *Raising Hell,* they embarked on what would be their most successful tour ever. The *Raising Hell* tour is still remembered as perhaps the greatest collection of talent ever assembled in one tour: Run-DMC, the Beastie Boys, LL Cool J, and a handful of lesser acts. The tour launched in Columbus, Georgia on May 21 and carried on for fifteen weeks into sixty-five cities, ending August 31 in Norfolk, Virginia. Late that year it made stops in Europe and Asia.

When Run-DMC needed to hire a crew for support on the road, Jay invited some of his Hollis buddies to come join the tour, and the payroll. He hired his friends Runny Ray and Garfield MacDonald as technical advisers to make sure the stage preparations were right. He hired his longtime friend Smith as a roadie, to help him set up his turntables. He hired his old pal Hurricane as security guard, to stand off-stage and ward off the inevitable stage crashers. Hurricane saw the offer of work as a lifeline. "I was still running the streets and Jay invited me to come with them," says Hurricane. "No way I was going to say no to that."

Hurricane accepted, and has always credited Jay not only with saving him from getting in dire trouble on the streets but also with giving him a career. In the middle of the tour the Beastie Boys' dj Dr. Dre unexpectedly quit. The Beasties needed help fast, and they offered the job to Hurricane. Hurricane had always hoped to be a dj but didn't feel as if he was ready. "I didn't want to do it. Then Jay came to me and said, 'Do it for me.' I took Jay's advice and the next thing I knew the Beastie Boys' *License to Ill* album came out and it was a hit, and I was right there with them. That changed my whole life. I went around the world on that."

Hurricane became DJ Hurricane and to this day has a flourishing solo career, including making records of his own, as well as a busy, lucrative schedule working concerts and parties. His successes allowed him to get out of Hollis and buy a new house in Atlanta for himself and his wife.

As the tour wore on Jay assumed more responsibility within Run-DMC. He became the group's de facto musical director, planning out the order of songs for each show, choosing which records to spin, setting the pace of the performance, keeping the proceedings in motion. It was almost inevitable that he would have such a strong hand in Run-DMC's live shows because he was the one who kept all the music in his head. Run and DMC may have been the ones doing the rapping, but Jay was the one who was holding them up. He *was* the show.

"Every rapper and dj today talks about the effect Run-DMC had on them," says MTV's Dave Sirulnick. "And the conversation always, always comes around to Jay." Chicago dj Bad Boy Bill attended some of the early shows and told *DJ Times,* "I remember going to a Run-

DMC concert and I was blown away by the entire show, but I was always focusing on Jay and how he was the foundation of the group. That really put the importance of the dj into perspective for me."

In the summer of 1986, in what is considered probably the greatest performance ever in hip hop music, Run-DMC sold out New York City's Madison Square Garden. This was the peak of Run-DMC's powers, and they were making $150,000 per night to headline a big arena show.

The music critic of *NY Talk* magazine raved about the *Raising Hell* tour. "As for Run-DMC's show, it is, despite the big time rock show additions of fancy lighting, cordless mikes, a bit of smoke, and a raised platform for Jam Master Jay's turntables, the rootsiest, most true-to-the-streets thing I've ever seen in an arena. Just two guys rapping, and one guy playing records, just like they used to do it in the parks and schoolyards and streets."

The tour was also significant as the start of what would become an important relationship between hip hop and corporate America. And once again, like almost all of Run-DMC's firsts, Jay would have a hand in it.

There was something special about coming to the Garden for Jay. For basketball fans like him it was the site of many Knicks victories, but it was also the pinnacle of the touring business, the same stage that had been walked by the Rolling Stones, Sly & the Family Stone, John Lennon, and James Brown. When he arrived early at the Garden through the backstage entrance that evening, Jay noticed a line of fans already snaking around one side of the building and massive crowds milling around the front hoping to score a scalped ticket. The concert was a big success, and halfway through the show, as they were about to launch into the hit song "My Adidas," Run stopped the concert in its tracks and asked: "How many people out there got Adidas?" Just like that a sea of hands shot in the air, and some 19,000 pairs of hands were all clutching Adidas. For Jay it was one of his greatest moments ever: Those were, indeed, his Adidas. He was also proud that he had passed the toughest test of his life. A dj could single-handedly rock an entire arena for two hours and send 19,000 fans home with a smile.

When Run came off stage that night, Angelo Anastasio, National Director of Entertainment Promotions for Adidas U.S.A., was watching from the sidelines and waiting. He was thrilled, and promised that Run-DMC would have its own contract to endorse the shoe. This was not the first time that Run had exhorted his audience to show him their Adidas. A month earlier in Philadelphia's Spectrum Arena, Run had done the same thing, and this time one of their managers had a videotape camera rolling. He wisely sent the tape to Adidas and a beautiful relationship was born.

Adidas was a German-based shoemaker that was launched by two brothers, Adi and Rudolf Dassler. The two brothers pioneered the athletic shoe business in Germany but for years had been unsuccessfully struggling to get a foothold in the giant U.S. market. The two brothers eventually had a falling out and decided to split the company in half. Adi founded Adidas, which was a play on his name, and Rudolf launched Puma. The two companies actually became rivals, competing for endorsements. The track star Edwin Moses and Run-DMC became Adidas endorsers, and the tennis star Boris Becker and soccer player Diego Maradona became Puma endorsers.

Not long after the Madison Square Garden event Run-DMC signed that contract with Adidas, worth $1.5 million, and Adidas began making four different styles modeled after suggestions from Jay and Run. It was the first known shoe deal for nonathletes. Needless to say, sales of shell-toe Adidas boomed. Later, Adidas would award Run-DMC with gold necklaces each with a small solid-gold Adidas shoe dangling from it. The shoes that Jay had first bought back on the Avenue in Hollis were now generating millions of dollars worldwide, and Jay was getting a piece of the action. To this day Adidas still sends shoes and gear to Run-DMC, all free. Corporate America and hip hop continued to grow closer, and before long, hip hop was being used to sell everything from soft drinks to blue jeans.

In 1988 Run-DMC shot an ad for Coca-Cola, that quintessentially American of corporate institutions. Looking at the ad today, your eye immediately goes to Jay, standing in the center, wearing a blue warm-up jacket, matching Kangol cap, black jeans, a gold wristwatch, and his gold Adidas shoe neck chain. Jay has a

funny, pinch-me-I-must-be-dreaming half-smile on
his face. There's an unwritten rule in hip hop that only
suckers cheese for a camera. But Jay looks so happy, so
proud of himself that for once the tough look that hip
hoppers practice in the mirror was pushed out and the
most genuine, heartfelt laugh seems to be sneaking
across his face.

Raising Hell's legendary music-making gave way to
legendary after-hours bacchanalias. The tour rolled
from city to city in an extended luxury bus equipped
with beds, televisions, stereos, and a refrigerator. The
personnel on board consisted of the three group members, Russell Simmons, their road manager Lyor
Cohen, Hurricane, Runny Ray, and a few assistants.
The bus was on the road most of the summer, stopping
in St. Louis, Detroit, Virginia, North Carolina, Indi-
anapolis, Philadelphia, Cleveland, L.A., and two dozen
more cities. Usually at the close of the show, someone
from one of the groups would announce to the audience the name of the hotel where they were staying,
and invite everyone to come on by for an after-party.
This is a time-honored tactic in rock and roll. By the
time the groups returned to the hotel the lobby was
filled with fans and groupies. And in scenes that
seemed to come out of a hip hop–style *Hard Day's
Night*, groupies chased Jay and Run and DMC down
hallways and into elevators and lined up outside their
rooms.

The parties were often more like sieges than celebrations. Run later recalled in his autobiography that "on any given night you could walk out into the hallway and see topless girls running from room to room." When the room got full Jay or D would lock the door. Opening it again was risky: Hordes of fans would try to push their way in. But for the guys it was worth it. Every city they stopped in they enjoyed the attentions of armies of groupies, which, when you're twenty-one, rich, famous, and single, is about as good as it gets.

Long Beach, California, however, did not go as planned. On August 17, as several thousand fans waited inside the Long Beach Arena for Run-DMC, two rival gangs began fighting it out right in the seats. The fight quickly grew out of control as gang members attacked each other with folding chairs and anything they could get their hands on. Backstage, Jay was getting ready for the show when he saw the mayhem going down out in the seats. Arena security guards were quickly over-whelmed and some of them ran for cover. A major riot was underway. Soon masses of rioters were crashing through the locked doors to the backstage area. Jay gathered up Run and DMC and they took refuge in a dressing room and barricaded the door. They could hear the rioters outside and were preparing to make their last stand when L.A. riot police finally showed up.

It took sixty riot police to finally clear the arena. Thirty-four fans wound up in the hospital. The next day Jay blamed the riot on the gangs, and defended Run-DMC against charges in the media that they fostered a climate of violence. "The gang thing was building up and they were going to meet at our show," Jay said. "We didn't have nothing to do with it. We had no control over it." He continued: "We stand for only positive things. So if 300 negative people come in a place how can you say they are with us positive people?"

Writing in the *Los Angeles Times* the next year, critic Robert Hilburn argued that Run-DMC's positive message was becoming drowned out in time-wasting finger-pointing. "All of the emphasis on the tension surrounding Run-DMC . . . is obscuring the real, liberating message of these shows: the racial integration of rock and roll."

Jay always saw hip hop as having room for everybody, and in the early days he more than once singled out some of the few white fans and thanked them for coming to their shows. Later in an interview with *USA Today*, he was asked if he believed the white rapper Eminem was stealing from black culture by "acting black." Jay bristled: "I think this is a racist question, and I don't have a bone of anything to think this way. Words are for everyone, man. Anyone can use any kind of words. I ignore stupidity, and I don't think he's trying to be stupid. He's just keeping it real."

In October 1988 the group made three high-profile tv appearances: They appeared on David Brenner's talk show *Nightlife*, where Brenner and DMC discussed the finer points of what makes cool shoes. Next they made an appearance on *Saturday Night Live*. The guest host that night was Spike Lee, who began his monologue by assuring the audience that Run-DMC was not the violent band that the media claimed they were. Then the camera cut to a scene backstage as producer Lorne Michaels was talking to Jay and accidentally stepped on Jay's Adidas. Jay and Run and DMC pummeled Michaels and then walked straight to the stage to perform a rousing "Walk This Way." Their next stop was *The Late Show Starring Joan Rivers* where they traded raps with the comedienne:

Well have you heard, I'm the first and number one
Not the best not the worst cause my name is Run
And I'm second cause I reckon that you want to see
An emcee like D inside the place to be
And have you heard that he is third and his name
   is Jay

The audience roared as Rivers got in one of her own:

I'm mama Joan and I'm here to say
I got my own show and I'm here to stay!

For most of that decade Run-DMC was the most famous hip hop band in the world, and Jay was the world's best-known dj. Despite the negative publicity picked up on the tours, Run-DMC recorded and released *Raising Hell* in 1986. That, too, was a turning point in hip hop and marked rap's crossover to tough drum machine beats and scratching effects. *Raising Hell* became Run-DMC's biggest hit ever and was for a time the biggest-selling album in rap history. It hit number Three on the *Billboard* charts and sold over 3 million copies, spurred by singles like "My Adidas" and "Walk This Way." "Walk This Way" became the first top-ten single in hip hop history, and Jay's role in its creation would add to his luster as the world's most famous dj.

When they started out it was a medium of 12-inch singles, no albums, and fifteen-minute live shows. In 1988, they were multiplatinum sellers—tours, MTV, kids from coast to coast memorizing lyrics.

And now hip hop culture was going around the world wearing Adidas.

eight

WALK THIS WAY

"We would have to find a hard beat to rap over," Jay once said in *BAM*. "We would take an old rock record and just open up, drum only followed by guitar, go to the other turntable and start another record so we could rap over this hard drum beat." That, in a nutshell, explains how Run-DMC's greatest hit, "Walk This Way," was born.

All songs start out as a single crystalline idea, a tight core of something good, and as they develop they accumulate layers of new ideas, always changing until they are finalized and released into the world. If you were to unravel the many layers of the 1986 version of "Walk This Way," you'd find Jay's fingerprints on that crystalline core. In early 1986 during the studio sessions for what would become the *Raising Hell* album, Jay one day came up with an idea. Shuffling through his collection of vinyl, which was at this point large enough to fill a railway freight car, he went straight to a 1975 Aerosmith album called *Toys in the Attic.* He began spinning his favorite cut, "Walk This Way." Jay had known the song for years and was intimately familiar with its every note: It was one of the records he spun in the parks in the early 1980s and he had always loved its crunching guitars and stuttering beat. Its extended break was ideal for rapping over, and the beat, well, man, did it have soul. Jay had become hip to the idea of rock as a rap tool way early, much the way early bebop musicians like Dizzy Gillespie and Charlie Parker would weave new music from the melodies of Gershwin and Cole Porter. One of his other favorite beats came from the somewhat obscure rock musician Billy Squier on his record "Big Beat," which Jay set up and spun for many an MC back in the days at Two-Fifth Park. Jay had cosmopolitan tastes: He was even known to listen to extreme punk rock occasionally, like the group Bad Brains, which, if you've ever had the pleasure, sounds like a horrible industrial accident. In the early days, to get the musical dynamics and velocity he craved for Run-DMC songs, Jay was frequently forced to resort to rock records. They were stuffed full of punchy beats. R&B and pop records were just too soft and squishy. A perceptive article in the British magazine *New Musical Express* in 1986 connected Jay directly with Run-DMC's hard-beat credentials. "Jam Master Jay has provided Run-DMC with breaks for over five years and originally introduced them to hard rock by using AC/DC and Aerosmith albums as part of his scratch repertoire."

Run later told VH1 that in the middle of the recording sessions for *Raising Hell* Jay suddenly put on "Walk This Way" and everybody's ears pricked up. "We got to the studio early and Jay pulled out the Aerosmith record, put it on, and we looped it up. Russell and Rick Rubin came in later and said, 'Oh, that's incredible! We've got to make this into a record.' " Jay remembered that when he first discovered the song, "Run used to rap over the beginning of that while I used to scratch it. That's where we got the guitar from with Run-DMC." This time around though, Jay had actually intended to just use the break, and nothing else, which they would drop in as part of another song. But producer Rick Rubin, one of the savviest minds in any studio, had an even better idea: He suggested that they re-record the entire song—and bring Aerosmith in on the process.

Rubin had long believed that the only reason rock and rap had not crossed paths yet was because of racism in the record business. The resistance, he suggested, came from white record executives who didn't like rap from the start. "It was so obvious that hip hop and rock were similar things," Rubin told me. In an interview in *Shark* magazine Rick explained his own reasons for making records like "Walk This Way." "I saw this void and started making those records, just because I was a fan and wanted them to exist." Run remembers going home that night still unable to understand what Tyler was singing on the song, and not at all sure how he was going to turn the words into his own style of rapping. "We didn't have any lyrics so they gave us the Aerosmith album and said go home and study this," he told VH-1. By the next day Joe came back flipping the rhymes around on his tongue and crowing about how much he liked the words to the song.

Aerosmith was a down-on-its-luck Boston rock and roll band that had abundant charisma, some great songs, but one major problem. Its lead singer, Steven Tyler, and guitarist, Joe Perry, had a fondness for drugs. The late 1970s and early 1980s had not been good to the band commercially, and they had disbanded and reluctantly reunited. It's still remarkable to remember that in the mid-1980s rock and rap were divided; radio stations that played rock never ever played rap, and vice versa. Rock and rap musicians didn't associate much either, except by accident occasionally at a festival like Live Aid. A few exceptional musicians like Jay seemed to have a foot in each world, but otherwise, rock and rap were parallel universes, seemingly fated to never meet.

When Aerosmith got the call from Rick Rubin, they had no idea who Run-DMC was, but, as Perry told writer Bill Adler, he had heard rap music blasting out of the bedroom of his thirteen-year-old stepson, so he figured why not. "It was new. It was fresh, in the rap sense of the term," Perry said. "I didn't go out and buy a bunch of rap records but I did get a sense of what was going on there." Plus, he had nothing much more to lose; he had a solo record that was going nowhere fast. Tyler didn't much care either but was spurred by the knowledge that there would be a check waiting for them at the end of the day. (Jay for his part later said he didn't have any idea who Aerosmith was either. He always thought that the group that recorded "Walk This Way" was the same name that he saw on the album cover *Toys in the Attic*.) Rubin made all the arrangements to bring Aerosmith down to New York, and in March 1986 they joined Run-DMC in a place called Magic Venture Studios.

There's a photo of that session that shows Rick Rubin and Jay in charge at the mixing board, with Tyler, Joe Perry, Run, and DMC milling around in the background looking somewhat lost. Observers present for the session that day remember that the chemistry between Aerosmith and Run-DMC wasn't even enough to strike a match with. Jay and Run looked at the slightly disheveled rockers with some sort of cross between flat disinterest and deep boredom. Tyler and Perry couldn't much care, either. Run couldn't remember which one was Steve and which one was Joe, and Joe had no idea which one was Run and which one was DMC. After some confusion they all got a little more comfortable with each other and the session stretched through most of that afternoon. A few bottles of Olde English were opened up and things loosened up nicely. Rubin told me: "I remember how intrigued Steven and Joe were watching Jay on the turntables manipulating their music. They were blown away."

The evident lack of chemistry between the two camps suddenly reversed itself when it came time to put something down on tape, and all the years of Run-DMC's experimentation with rock and rap suddenly came together to produce some positively combustible results. It turned into a huge hit for the group, and Aerosmith would catch a ride on the slipstream of "Walk This Way," too. Their career lifted off once again, as did much of classic rock, and more hits followed. In the mid-1990s they signed a multimillion-dollar deal with Sony Music and enjoyed a new wave of popularity. "Walk This Way" sounded a lot like Aerosmith's original, but with Jay's pronounced scratching pouncing on the famous opening drum pattern, you immediately know you're in for a different kind of ride. Run and DMC interject with their patented cross-talk and their vocals never sounded more impudent and blustery—or better. Tyler's voice, a banshee's shriek, rides above it all, and the result is an uncommon kind of magic.

The union of rock and rap was like two great rivers meeting, and Jay, you might say, had his hand in the waters. On August 16, 1986, the single appeared on record-store shelves. The record-buying public gobbled it up hungrily. Rick Rubin was correct—there were obviously hundreds of thousands of fans who had been waiting for something like this. "Walk This Way" leaped up the charts and it dragged the *Raising Hell* album along with it. "Walk This Way" topped out at No. 4 on the singles chart and the album would climb as high as No. 3. It took seventy-one weeks before it would finally sink off the charts, a triumph of considerable proportions.

In its wake, both pop and rap radio were forced to rethink their formats. The song masterfully gave each camp something to work with, and was an especially welcome lifeline for pop radio stations that had long been eager to find a way into the coming rap explosion but were hemmed in by format restrictions. Until that moment the division between rock and hip hop was still very clear on a commercial level. Rock radio never played hip hop and hip hop was limited to a few outlets, among them KDAY in Los Angeles, which had begun playing virtually nothing but hip hop in 1984. Now station after station played "Walk This Way." The song has been called a bridge into the mainstream, and MTV's Dave Sirulnick even called it "a Golden Gate Bridge into the mainstream."

Raising Hell also spawned two minor hit singles, "You Be Illin' " and "It's Tricky," which sampled a rock guitar lick from "My Sharona" by the new wave band the Knack. *Rolling Stone* magazine instantly grasped the significance of the *Raising Hell* album. In a December 1986 article the rock and roll journal lauded Run-DMC lavishly, referring to the album as "a master blast of heavy metal," and credited Run-DMC with changing hip hop and rock in one scratch as "New York's mightiest mouths took their megamix of street corner braggadocio and turntable superscratch into the Top

Ten." Continuing, the magazine then hit on a crucial point: "Without backing down an inch to urban contemporary crossover pressure, Run-DMC stormed into white America's living rooms."

Raising Hell caught another honor: It received a Grammy nomination for "Best R&B performance by a Duo or Group with Vocal." This was, of course, before Grammy recognized a rap music category.

Jay was feeling his power. In an interview in the *Washington Post* not long afterward, he was uncharacteristically ungenerous toward the Purple Majesty of R&B, and also to the pashas who control the radio business. "I feel we're a bigger act than Prince is," Jay crowed. "I feel that Run-DMC is much hipper." He went on to express frustration with radio, which in all fairness had never supported them. "We would sell five times more records with radio play," Jay griped. "Play my record enough for everybody to like it. And we'll take over." Later, as he looked back, Jam Master Jay was humble about his key role in the song that revolutionized rock and rap. "We were hip hop guys who took some rock and roll and blended it 'cause it was good music. Good music is just good music," he said to a reporter from the Cornell *Daily Sun*. "I feel proud and honored to still have fun with it."

The revolution that was touched off by the "Walk This Way" single was carried even further into the consciousness of America when the music video was released a few months later. Six weeks after *Raising Hell* came out video director Jon Small called up Aerosmith to pitch them a concept for a music video. Small had just come off a rather high-profile success shooting the video for newcomer Whitney Houston's "The Greatest Love of All" and a few days later happened to be sharing an elevator with Profile Records' Steve Plotnicki. It just so happened that Plotnicki had just seen the Whitney video and loved it. Before the elevator doors opened Plotnicki offered Small a job directing the video for a new Run-DMC single called "Walk This Way."

Rap videos were still mostly new in 1986 and most record executives viewed the possibility of reaching a large rap audience with them as chancy at best. But more and more the video seemed to be gaining success working as a pop marketing tool so rap labels continued making them, but always on the cheap. There were plenty of other reasons why they were considered high risk—foremost among them that MTV was hardly enthusiastic about rap music then. The only music channel in America turned down many hip hop videos, sometimes for artistic reasons, other times because they insisted that their audience's appetite was really for rock and metal.

Small took the job. The budget that he was given for the shoot—$60,000—seems so tiny now that it might not even cover the cost of cheese trays and soft drinks at some big video shoots today. ("Scream," a 1995 Michael Jackson video costarring his sister Janet, cost $1 million.) There was another problem. Small had no idea who Run-DMC was, nor did he know anything about any rap group for that matter. He was about as far from a rap aficionado as you could get. So he went out and bought some rap records, listened to them, and then one day he hopped on a subway train and rode it all day. He rolled through Queens, Harlem, the Bronx, and Brooklyn. He got out on 125th Street and then the Grand Concourse and on Jamaica Avenue and in Bedford-Stuyvesant. He walked up and down the streets where Run-DMC's fans and imitators lived. He listened to the sounds that were blaring from car radios and out the doors of storefront shops. Small observed young hip hop fans—he saw and memorized their gestures, their look, their language, the streetwise swagger, the shoes without laces. It was the best a rock and roll–raised white guy clueless about hip hop could do on short notice.

Jon Small is one of the few people in the music business to have worked on both sides of the camera. Before he directed music videos, he made his living as a musician. Small worked as a touring drummer for more than a decade, playing seven years with Billy Joel and off and on with a variety of other big-name groups, including the Edgar Winter Band, the Doobie Brothers, and the Kinks. His drumming career ended abruptly when he seriously injured his leg in a motorcycle accident. When he got out of the hospital he decided to open up a small musician management company. When that was successful he started a record label, and one day he got a call from a promoter asking him if he had a video for one of his artists. He didn't, so he wound up shooting one himself for $685, and his new career was born.

Small wrote up a treatment for "Walk This Way" that visualized the two groups practicing in studios separated by a wall, and then breaking down that wall and performing together. Location scouts found a perfect site, the grand old Park Theater in Union, New Jersey. But according to Small, Tim Collins, Aerosmith's manager, was positively afraid to allow his clients to come to New York. The band had been clean for about six months and Collins was afraid that left alone in Sin City they would be tempted to end their sobriety. "They'll be shooting dope if I let them go to NYC by themselves," Small remembered Collins saying. Small had a solution: He booked the band hotel rooms in New Jersey and hired a couple of round-the-clock bodyguards to keep an eye on them and make sure they stayed clear of any trouble.

Jay and Run and DMC arrived early on the first day of the two-day shoot. It was their first big video and they didn't know any better. Aerosmith showed up sometime that afternoon. Run-DMC set up in an upstairs dressing room while downstairs in the basement Aerosmith and a few friends hung out, partying. Run and DMC were suspicious of the director, afraid that he might somehow make them look stupid. Small quickly realized that if he wanted to get them to do anything without a lot of persuasion, it had to go through Jay first. When Small was shooting the now iconic close-up shot of the guys in their three sets of laceless Adidas doing a little march as they come down a stairstep, DMC balked, fearful that he might fall. A few words from Jay and everything was ironed out. When Small asked Run to rub his nose in that cool way that he did, Run looked at him like he had two heads. "Rub your nose, Run," said Jay, and then it was cool, too. When Small told them to bang on the wall, they both looked over at Jay. Run and DMC relied on Jay as their cool filter. If it got past Jay, it was cool.

But Small remembers that Jay and Run and DMC "were totally relaxed on camera. They were stars right from the top. They knew who they were and you didn't have to tell them how to perform." At the end of the first day, which lasted eighteen hours, Run and DMC sat on the stairs leaning against each other, both drifting off to sleep. Around 4 A.M. Steven Tyler walked in wide awake and attempted to start a conversation with them. Run and DMC just shut their eyes and ignored him.

The climax scene of the video was shot before a live audience of 1,500 or so teenagers, who piled into the theater in response to an open call on the radio the previous day. Small had purposely gathered a mixed crowd of black and white kids to give the scene a coming-together look, and you can see the kids teeming and swaying in the background. The video opens with Aerosmith and Run-DMC rehearsing in side-by-side studios separated by a thin wall. Aerosmith is performing "Walk This Way" so loudly that Run, next door, can't hear himself. "Yo, keep it down in there!" shouts Jay from behind his bank of turntables, as Run first pounds on the wall, then wheels a giant speaker over, aims it at the wall, and cranks it up high. Now Run-DMC is rapping to "Walk This Way" and blasting out Tyler, who is fed up and getting more frustrated by the second. When he can't stand it anymore he lays into the wall. What Small didn't tell Tyler is the prop wall was sturdily built, so Tyler had to really bang it convincingly to make a dent in it.

After a few sharp blows from his microphone stand he breaks a hole through, and as light streams in from the other side, he juts his head through to see Run-DMC looking back at him. Cut away and the two groups are now joined together on a stage performing the song in front of a live audience that is roaring wildly. The wall between rock and rap had come tumbling down, and the results were glorious. Tyler and DMC and Run lock arms and dance in sync, a funny little shuffle step, that like so much of the video is now immortalized. MTV loved it and put it in heavy rotation for months. It recently appeared on MTV's rankings of the most popular videos of all time, coming in only behind Peter Gabriel's "Sledgehammer." "Walk This Way" went down in the canon of Run-DMC, a legacy hit that they could perform every night from now until eternity.

For the generation of adults whose teen years fell between 1980 and 1990, seeing Run-DMC's "Walk This Way" music video for the first time had the same kind of electrifying effect that the Beatles performing on the *Ed Sullivan Show* had for young Baby Boomers in 1964. The Beatles inspired legions of kids to pick up

guitars and form bands and view pop music with a respect that had never before existed. Two decades later
the sight of Jam Master Jay working the turntables
while Run and DMC and Aerosmith's Steven Tyler
danced made a whole new generation run to their
turntables, and it opened a door to a world of possibilities made real by blending rap with rock. Lots of cool
kids still wanted to grow up to play guitar, but after
"Walk This Way" first ran on MTV in 1986, many of
them decided that becoming a dj was cooler. And their
role model was Jam Master Jay.

The dj was a well-established figure in hip hop by
1986, but to most of mainstream America hip hop
music was still over the horizon. A dj was still the guy
who plays the music heard on your radio dial. Until the
music's explosive growth in the late 1990s, in fact, hip
hop's reach was quite limited. Pop radio stations,
which commanded the vast majority of ears, never
played it. Most of them are still bound by tightly controlled playlists selected not by a dj but by suits in the
marketing department. They base their lists on listener
research, not artistic merit. The concert business was
warming up to hip hop, but slowly. Some powerful
promoters believed rap concerts attracted gangs and
triggered violence, and there were incidents in Los Angeles and New York that appeared to back them up.
Television treated hip hop as if it was mostly nonexis-
tent. MTV aired Run-DMC's "Rock Box" video in 1983
but not much else after that besides Michael Jackson.

In the early 1980s, MTV's distribution was far smaller than it is now. In fact, when "Rock Box" and "Walk This Way" went out over MTV's cable system, Run and Jay and DMC couldn't watch it at home because Queens was not yet wired for cable. So as the great bulk of America that lives outside of New York and Los Angeles slowly awakened to the music revolution that was on their doorstep, the first dj to alter the old consciousness was Jam Master Jay. His style was not incredibly revolutionary, but he was the first one to carry it forward. "He single-handedly pretty much created the dj industry, not as far as his technical innovations or being the first to do it, but as far as bringing the whole concept to the people worldwide," said dj Scott Hardkiss in the magazine *DJ Times.* Jim Tremayne, editor of *DJ Times,* says, "Jay was the first one many of us saw on tv. He brought that wider consciousness about the dj."

There were other djs who were probably more famous, like Grandmaster Flash, or more experienced, like Davy DMX, but for millions of future hip hop fans Jay was the first figure they saw on their tv sets. When they looked at Run-DMC and asked themselves, "Where's the band?" Jam Master Jay answered them with a flourish on the turntables. Jay "showed everyone you could have a one-man band," said Scott Hardkiss in *DJ Times,* "an entire rhythm section who used two record players to play all the drums, bass guitars, keyboards, and percussion, and the sound he brought to the group of just the stripped-down beats with stabs of guitar infused hip hop with the energy of rock and roll; we all know where that led to."

A whole generation of musicians who rose to fame in the mid-'90s have all credited "Walk This Way" with introducing that spark in their life.

In Detroit, Bob Ritchie was watching. Ritchie later became famous as the rap-rocker Kid Rock and would share a stage with Run-DMC on their final tour.

In Bakersfield, California, so was Jonathan Davis. Davis founded Korn, the rap metal band that hit it big with its guitar-based rap-rock.

At home in suburban Chicago, Tom Morello was watching, too. Later as lead guitarist for Rage Against the Machine, the exceptional rap-rock band of the late '90s, he displayed a thorough knowledge of early Run-DMC tracks and a fluidity with both rap and rock intricacies.

Fred Durst, the lead singer of the enormously popular rap-metal act Limp Bizkit, told VH1 that Run-DMC "made hip hop music that the whole world could get. They like made a lot [of] white people that wouldn't have bothered 'cause maybe they didn't get it or didn't want to get it. But they made it happen and I guess I was one of those people."

And on the other side of Detroit, Marshall Mathers was watching. Years later, when he became Eminem, he said that one of his first memories of hip hop was watching Jam Master Jay scratching.

Rap-rock is now no longer considered an offshoot, but a mainstream genre in its own right.

*   *   *

As the "Walk This Way" generation came of age in the 1990s, so did deejaying. A dj culture and a dj industry arose to support it, blooming around the globe, and spread out along an archipelago of studios and nightclubs in hotspots like London and Manchester, New York and Los Angeles, Paris, Berlin, and Madrid. Sure, a part of the dj boom was fed by disco and later house music (a frenetically paced dance music that originated in Chicago), but dance dj's have always been around. Furthermore, their popularity generally remained tied to the dance floor. Hip hop dj's enjoyed a wider creative compass, and became the fathers of the new phenomenon of dj's as solo artists, sometimes called "turntablists." "Jay really stimulated the industry, the art of deejaying, the buying and selling of dj equipment," says Tremayne. "The industry would never be where it is today without his influence." Jay carefully maintained his visibility—appearing at dj conventions and showcases regularly. He benefited from this, but so did the dj's who followed his path. For the first time they were taken seriously as musicians and a few of them, like Moby, Funkmaster Flex, and Fatboy Slim, gathered so much fame that they became familiar even to people who don't listen to or like hip hop.

Business accelerated: dj's were in demand and began appearing in tv commercials and making soundtracks for movies. The best dj's, whether it was producing a record or touring with a group or just spinning records at a club, began making a very good living: $25,000 or more for a night's work. Some dj's became so in demand that they traveled by luxury private bus, just like musicians. And a few, like Funkmaster Flex in New York City, have parlayed dj work into a small business empire. Flex dj's NYC's most popular radio show, makes his own records, and produces other acts on the side.

But if you trace back the artistic DNA of just about any dj, chances are it will lead back to Jam Master Jay.

Dj Michael Sansone of New York explained that "Jay opened the door and let the rest of America join the party. Hip hop might still be a curious novelty," he told *DJ Times*, "like current day jazz or an underground, word of mouth phenomenon like hardcore punk if these guys hadn't found a way to merge their black-as-asphalt rap with a backbeat straight out of the white American mainstream. As was the case with every pop musical style that came before, whether jump blues/hillbilly boogie of the 40's, Chess/Sun rock-n-roll of the 50's, Stax/Fame soul of the 60's, or the Prince/P-Funk disco stew of the 70's and early 80's; when ya integrate, ya propagate, and then all hell breaks loose. And it only took about 10 seconds on the intro to 'Walk This Way,' Run-DMC style, for everyone else to get it."

Dj Spinderella, the gorgeous dj who spun records for the '90s female hip hop trio Salt-N-Pepa, says Jay's popularity also alerted record labels that you probably can't find better talent scouts and judges of what's hot and what's not than a dj. After all, dj's spend a lot of time in clubs, in the presence of large crowds, and they get to see what works and what doesn't. Many record labels now rely on dj's to give them an edge. They employ dj's to act as their eyes and ears and early warning system, so they can get a jump on trends before the competition does.

Jay brought something new to the job description that will always be there, Spin told me. "Just like Biggie and Tupac kind of immortalized the MC, Jam Master Jay did the same for the dj. He put a light on the dj, put him on a pedestal, and that helped all of us," says Spin. "I just loved the chops he had, too, the chukka chukka chukka chukka boom! Chukka chukka chukka chukka chukka boom! His signature moves were just great and undeniable. I utilize his 'Peter Piper' in my own show. Jay was doing exactly what I want to do." Spin has built a flourishing career for herself as a dj since leaving Salt-N-Pepa, pulling down thousands of dollars a night and traveling the world to work in England, Australia, and elsewhere. "It wasn't this way before Jay's generation," she says. One of the world hot spots for dj's and hip hop now is Japan, she says. "There's a massive hip hop community there and they have their own dj's and their own MC's and it's just growing massively. They absolutely love hip hop culture. I think Jay visited there in the '80s and helped kick that whole thing off."

nine

GO YOUR OWN WAY

Ten years from now I'd like to have a
boomin' record company and be on stage.
I'll be 30-something so my music will be a
lot different, but I'll never give up, I like
doing this!

—Jam Master Jay, to the magazine *Hip Hop
Connection*, December 1990

How many of us can say that we go out every day
and live our dreams as faithfully as Jam Master
Jay once predicted for himself?

How many of us not just dare to dream the dream
but then also have what it takes when we wake up and
get out of bed to go do what's needed to really make it
happen?

Jam Master Jay did, and perhaps that's why he
seemed so content, so optimistic when he struck out
on his own. He didn't see himself performing with
Run-DMC and flying off to do dj shows around the
world forever. He and Terri had talked it over, and Jay's
next plan was to build his own businesses up from the
inside, to carve out a space for himself as an executive
so he could help the next generation of kids make a
mark while he watched from behind a desk. "He did

say by the age of forty-five that he needed to start settling down and be a big business person behind the scene," his wife, Terri, said about her husband in a conversation with VH-1 in 1999.

Maybe it was something left over from his days as a struggling dj, or perhaps it was deeper, an artifact from his memories growing up with never more than a few bucks in his pocket. Jay was a go-getter who lived life in motion, making connections and always scaring up work, even when things got tight. "Jay always had his own thing going, his own rep, his own clientele," says Bill Adler, who knew him for two decades. "He was always juggling a lot of different things at once."

In the ghetto people like that are called hustlers; in nicer neighborhoods they call them entrepreneurs. Jay's entrepreneurial side showed itself most clearly when business began to slow down for Run-DMC in the late 1980s and early 1990s, and legal entanglements sidelined them for a time. Jay wisely used his celebrity as a platform to reach out into other ventures. This would come in handy, because as Run-DMC's touring tapered off, they became more dependent on record royalties, and as record sales rose and then fell, so did their income.

Although all three members of the group earned handsome money and lived well beyond what might be called "comfortable," none got rich like the fabulously wealthy executives who sold their music. Why? The deal their management got for them with Profile Records gave the three of them 10 percent of retail sales of their records. That could be worth a couple of hundred thousand dollars apiece some years, and in other years, much less. Run-DMC's publishing rights, the lucrative aftermarket that provides continuing income years after a record comes out, is owned by Steve Plotnicki, the former head of Profile.

Ownership of music is generally divvied up like this: When you go into a record store and plop down $14.99 for a disc, you are actually buying three different things.

First, you are buying the physical record itself, the compact disc, the piece of plastic that holds the sound. That is usually owned by a record company.

Second, you are buying the particular song that is on that record. That is usually owned by the songwriter, but not always.

Third, you are buying that particular performance of that song, and that is usually owned by the performer on the album cover.

This is why popular songwriters who manage to keep ownership of their work can become wealthy, like Burt Bacharach or Alanis Morissette or Stevie Wonder or Sting. A popular song can be better than gold. If you've ever wondered how your favorite musician survives just putting out one album every four years, it's because well after a hit album is released, the checks keep on coming. A few blockbuster classics like Pink Floyd's *Dark Side of the Moon* or Bob Marley's *Legend* continue to sell year-in and year-out, sometimes as many as 10,000 copies a week. That's amazing when you realize that when *Dark Side of the Moon* first appeared, Richard Nixon was in the White House, and Bill Clinton was just fresh out of Oxford.

Every time a record is sold, a royalty is paid out to the owners of its copyrights, with the biggest share going to the owners of the song itself. So the next time you turn on the tv and realize that the jingle used in a commercial to hawk soda or detergent is actually a familiar oldie, you can bet that somebody somewhere just got cut a big check. That's why Michael Jackson paid $47 million in 1985 for a large stake in Northern Songs, a portion of the song catalog of John Lennon and Paul McCartney. The future earning power of those hits, which include songs like "Revolution" and hundreds of others, is unlimited. In 1986 Nike paid Jackson a fee estimated in the hundreds of thousands of dollars for the use of "Revolution" in a controversial tv ad promoting one of its sport shoes. The use of a Beatles song—which many Baby Boomers have invested with special emotional and nostalgic meaning—seemed offensive at first (the surviving Beatles sued Capitol Records and Jackson), especially when used to plug overpriced sneakers. Today deals like that are routine.

It was a fight over royalties that sidetracked Run-DMC's recording career at a critical crossroads. In 1988 Russell Simmons sued Profile Records to get a bigger percentage of those royalties and to free Run-DMC from its contract there. It's customary in the record business for highly successful acts to renegotiate their terms once they begin earning large sums of money for a record label. Simmons believed that he could get a better deal for them at another label, but Profile, not surprisingly, balked. Run-DMC was single-handedly responsible for 90 percent of their sales. The legal fight distracted the group at the worst possible time: The blockbuster success of *Raising Hell* had raised expectations among its growing fan base for a quick follow-up. But the group's next two albums were recorded under a cloud of discontent, and showed it. *Tougher Than Leather* (1988) and *Back from Hell* (1990) had little of the freshness of their earlier albums, and fans responded less than enthusiastically. The lawsuit was finally settled in favor of Profile. Run-DMC remained at the label but would release only two albums during the entire decade of the 1990s.

While all this legal infighting was preoccupying Run-DMC, hip hop was changing. Rappers began seizing the spotlight, leaving the first wave of dj's in the shadows. And in 1989 the maturing of West Coast hip hop announced itself when a group of Los Angeles rappers going by the name N.W.A made their mark with a stunning record called *Straight Outta Compton*. That record was more angry and explicit than anything that had come before, and it portrayed a luridly exciting world of hardened street gangs and corrupt cops. It was musically sophisticated. It had, in one stroke, upped the stakes for any rapper who believed he had a story worth telling. A few years later, the record would be recognized as the start of hip hop's most popular but troubling genre: gangsta rap.

N.W.A took Run-DMC's street-styled image and boiled off all the humor. In its place were lyrics about drive-by shootings and beat-downs of enemies, and the record was grim and rageful and unrelenting. It quickly found an audience and a legion of imitators.

As the prospects for Run-DMC dimmed a bit, Jay was the best prepared to handle the adverse weather. He was producing records now, he had opened his own record label, he bought a studio, and he began pulling down good money on the side, shooting instructional videos for aspiring dj's and spinning records in nightclubs. This busy regimen of moonlighting kept his career vital when Run and DMC ran into personal troubles that threatened to break up the group. Pressures began building when *Tougher Than Leather* became their first album to sell below expectations.

A tour of 20,000-seat arenas went out in 1988, but it was only half-filled most nights. It didn't help that the group also threw away a large chunk of their own money financing a disastrous film by the same name. *Tougher Than Leather* starred Run-DMC and was directed by Rick Rubin. It was intended to be an edgy adventure-farce, along the lines of action flicks like *48 Hours* or *The Mack* or *Rambo*. The plot was pure pulp: Runny Ray, Run-DMC's friend and roadie, is shot and killed backstage after a show, along with a known drug dealer. Police decide that the two killed each other over a drug deal. Run-DMC realize that someone has set

Runny Ray up, so they investigate themselves and solve the murder to clear Runny's name.

But when it was finished and screened for critics, it turned out to be amateurishly awful, and its vivid, repetitive violence repelled even the hardest of hard-core hip hop fans. I was present at one of those early screenings, and I recall that Jay was one of the few bright spots of the film. He delivered his lines—even those that seemed to have been cobbled right out of a block of wood—with a naturalistic zing. He was no Denzel Washington, but then again, in 1988, neither yet was Denzel Washington. The film had a mercifully short run in theaters. The initial cost of making the movie started out at $300,000, but after a long string of bungles and cost overruns it ballooned to $700,000 before wrapping. *Tougher Than Leather* then sat on the shelf for nearly a year before a distributor finally picked it up. The strain of that fiasco caused Run and DMC and Jay to begin to drift apart.

Jay plunged deeper into his own schedule, but for Run and DMC things only got worse. On August 9, 1991, Run-DMC performed a concert in Cleveland and stayed overnight at a downtown hotel. As was custom, that night they threw a party on their hotel room floor and entertained single ladies from several surrounding counties. The next day a twenty-two-year-old Cleveland woman and rap fan came forward with a stunning accusation: After attending the concert she had come to Run's room in hopes of getting an autograph, but instead of giving her an autograph, Run had raped her, she said. Police conducted a search of the room and found condoms and marijuana. Run denied every aspect of her tale, calling it "ridiculous and untrue," and swore that he did not even recall meeting her, let alone touching her. Two weeks later the district attorney handed up an indictment anyway on three counts of rape and one count of kidnapping. Run pled not guilty.

That same month Mike Tyson was convicted of raping a beauty pageant contestant in Indiana. Run was all nerves as he watched Iron Mike on the evening news in manacles as he was being escorted into prison. Run's luck changed though. Just hours before the trial was to start, a judge threw out the case, when the woman refused to testify and the prosecutor said he had no other evidence to support the charges. Run's lawyers later said the woman had made another phony rape allegation in the past.

Still, the damage to Run was considerable: By the time he exhaled and walked out of court free, he had already been forced to spend hundreds of thousands of dollars for his defense. He had been raked over and again in the newspapers. And the emotional strain caused his marriage to collapse: He and his wife separated and later divorced.

Not long after Run's ordeal, DMC revealed that he was struggling with alcoholism, and had been doing so for years. He admitted that he sometimes drank as many as eight 40-ounce bottles of beer a day. His preference had always been the potent malt liquor Olde

English 800. Olde English is legendary for its skunky flavor and powerful kick, and DMC had made a habit of swigging his way through bottle upon bottle during recording sessions, video tapings, anywhere. His habit got so bad that DMC eventually stopped eating when he realized he could drink more beer if his stomach was empty.

Hopped-up on Olde English one night in an Atlanta nightclub, he got into a brawl with a couple of bouncers that carried on out into the street. When an Atlanta police officer was sent in to break it up, DMC tried to take him on too. DMC wound up on the short end of that fight and was hauled away handcuffed and under arrest for assaulting an officer. And to boot, his face and head were both badly bruised during the fisticuffs. One morning, he woke up feeling extreme back pain. At the hospital a doctor told him he had severe alcoholic pancreatitis brought on by his drinking and that he must give up alcohol right away, or risk dying.

DMC would recover only to get more bad news. Years and years of screaming in concerts and on records had damaged his vocal cords and he could no longer rap in the booming raised-pitch shout that once interlocked so perfectly with Run's voice. For months, though, he didn't know what was happening.

A voice is the most complex instrument in the world and the most difficult to repair when something goes wrong with it. When he could no longer hit the same notes as before, DMC's record label became concerned and sent him to a psychiatrist. DMC finally realized he was losing his psychological desire to keep rapping. He walked out during the sessions for Run-DMC's *Crown Royal* album in 2000, and Run and Jay used older recordings and electronic sleight-of-hand to cover up the missing spots.

Run and DMC both later became born-again Christians, and Run became an ordained minister. "When you're not of sound mind nothing flows," Run later told *The Source* magazine. "If you came back then, it would have been eerie; I was buggin', D was somewhere else, and Jay was just trying to hold it all together."

Jay had two traumatic events temporarily disrupt his life, too. On Christmas night 1987 he and a couple of friends left the Red Parrot nightclub in Manhattan and were driving in Jay's Jeep down the West Side Highway when another car came suddenly hurtling at him, speeding on the wrong side of the road. Jay veered to the right in an attempt to get clear but the oncoming car followed him. The impact struck his Jeep head-on. Jay was thrown forward and his head went through the windshield, knocking him unconscious. The shattered glass left a nasty cut on his forehead, and permanent scars near his hairline and on his legs. The other passengers in the car, members of a band Jay was working with called Seriouslee Fine, were also injured, but none seriously.

Eventually Jay's pals at the club wondered what had happened to him and came looking. They saw flashing lights and then spotted his wrecked Jeep on the side of the highway. They found him lying on a bed in a hospital emergency room. Jay stayed in the hospital for the next few days.

Precisely a year later, Jay was exiting the Tunnel nightclub in Manhattan just as a fight broke out between two men who had been lingering outside the club's door. One of them pulled a gun and fired off some shots. "I'm out partying and I get blasted in the leg," Jay told VH-1. "I'm looking around to see where the shots are coming from and 'Pop, pop, I'm shot.' "

There was plenty of blood flowing from the bullet hole, but Jay managed to drive himself to the same hospital emergency room where he'd spent his last Christmas night. As he limped in he recognized the same doctor and the same nurse on duty, and they stared as he entered and said, "Jay! Not you again." He was lucky; the wound left no permanent injury.

None of this, however, slowed down Jay's solo career, which was now switching into high gear. He was flying around the world doing dj club gigs. He even opened up a dj referral service, because inevitably while doing a gig in Munich or Berlin, he'd get a call from Frankfurt asking him to show up the next day. The money was good—sometimes $10,000 or more a night—but he didn't have the spontaneity he once had. With a referral service, club promoters could go on line and find someone in an instant. Closer to home, Jay had also become an in-demand studio producer, and got steady work producing records for a string of high-profile acts like Roxanne, an early hip hop star; Public Enemy, the firebrand political rap group led by Chuck D; Slick Rick, an eye-patch-wearing British expatriate whose singsongy style created a sensation; and Shinehead, a reggae-rapper from London via the Bronx.

Jay also produced a new act that was a discovery of his own called Onyx. Onyx, a hard-core hip hop group, hit it big in 1993 with their debut entitled *Bacdafucup,* a smash hit that sold 2 million copies. Jay was able to use his Onyx success as a calling card at any record label in New York. Whenever he had an idea or proposal and wanted to sit down with somebody at a label who could make a decision, the door was open.

Around 1988 Jay formed a production company with Davy D, his old Hollis mentor, and for a couple of years they produced records for the hip hop group the Afros (whose main members were Hollis stalwarts Hurricane and Cool T) as well as Seriouslee Fine, a trio of MCs. The Afros showed the most promise and a few years later when Jay launched his own label, JMJ Records, as part of a joint venture with Russell Simmons's Rush Management, he brought the Afros with him and released their 1991 debut, *Kickin' Afrolistics.* Their record scored a moderate success. Jay also signed a female rapper by the name of Sugar, and he even briefly drew up plans for a line of hip hop–influenced clothing (years before Russell Simmons's Phat Farm and P. Diddy's Sean John lines had even stitched their first seam), although it did not get very far. Run and

DMC would open their own label, too, but it would quickly fade.

Jay continued pushing ahead. Around 1995 he scraped together several thousand dollars and purchased his own studio at the corner of Archer and Jamaica avenues in Queens. That studio burned down and took all his equipment with it, but in 1999 he found another one, this time on Merrick Boulevard. It was a smart move. Studio time is one of the biggest expenses in recording, sometimes running as much as $500 an hour, depending on demand and how well equipped a facility it is. Whenever a group goes into a studio to record an album for a record label, you can bet that there's a bean counter lurking nearby, tallying up the hours and ready to shut things down if the bill runs too high. For many musicians that sort of thing is nothing less than a bane because as they see it, creativity doesn't wear a wristwatch. Sometimes the best ideas come at 3 A.M., just when everyone is on the verge of collapse. Other times it may come over a bowl of cereal on Sunday morning. That's just the way it works, and for people like Jay, the juices flow whenever they happen to be in the mood, and having your own place to record can make life that much easier.

Jay was what is known in the business as a studio rat. That may sound derogatory but it's not. A studio rat, like a gym rat or a mall rat, is a person who spends lots of time in one place doing one thing. In music the phrase describes anyone from mixing-board whiz kids like Dr. Dre to Andy Slater, now head of Capitol

Records: tech-oriented music heads who live for the endless late-night hours perfecting songs, experimenting with sounds, and shooting the bull as they wait for their creative muse to come through the door.

P. Diddy, who has for years owned his own studio, Daddy's House, in Manhattan, once told me that buying a studio was one of the best moves he ever made. If his career as a solo artist were to ever dry up, he said, he could always fall back on the income the studio generates every month in rental fees. And if for some reason he ever lost control of his record label, or otherwise hit on lean times, he could always go to the studio and start from scratch. It's a lesson as old as Karl Marx: ownership of the means of production. As of this writing Puffy recently moved his Bad Boy Records from its home at BMG Music, where he had been for most of the last decade, because of BMG's cost cutting. After months of difficult shopping for a new corporate partner, he signed on with Universal Music Group in early 2003. But his studio is doing just fine.

The space that Jay bought was not fancy by any means, but it did the trick perfectly. Studio 24/7, as Jay named it, faces Merrick Boulevard, a busy corridor that runs between Jamaica and Hollis. Inside, it has a sound-proof recording room with control panels for all the equipment, and an outer lounge area for relaxing. Before he bought the studio, Jay asked John King, his old friend from Chungking Studio, to come out, have a look, and make some recommendations about the best equipment to purchase. Studios may be profitable businesses, but they take lots of up-front cash to get them going. King estimated that Jay had at least $300,000 (and possibly a lot more if you throw in the cost of the real estate) invested in the studio, a number that caused him some worry. Said King, "I didn't like the building much, I felt it was not secure. It was not an environment I would put a lot of expensive equipment in. It didn't seem safe."

In the neighborhood, however, 24/7 caught on instantly and was almost always in use. Jay was a soft touch when it came to allowing rappers with big dreams and small wallets a chance to get time on the equipment to polish up a demo or get their ideas down on tape. He gave up thousands of dollars in fees that way but he felt good about cutting people a break. Sometimes this was smart business because it was a way of getting first crack at any grassroots talent that might be sprouting—talent that he could produce, for a fee, or perhaps sign to his own record label. But as with any business, those moments of raw talent came along rarely, and the days in between are filled with the entire range from the average to the mediocre.

Jay hired some associates to help him out. He was working closely with Randy Allen, a Hollis kid from way back, and Randy had brought along his sister, Lydia High, to handle studio bookkeeping and day-to-day things that Jay's business needed done. Chuck D remembers that "Jay hated red tape. He just liked to get things done without a lot of talk. But there was always paperwork and problems and complications. Sometimes the business side of music frustrated him." If there was one less thing to worry about by farming out responsibility, Jay felt, that was good. Still, the studio was Jay's haven and his favorite place to be. He proved his own ear for talent was still sharp when in early 2002 he produced some sessions for an unknown rapper from Queens called 50 Cent. 50 Cent, whose real name is Curtis Jackson, went on to sign with Eminem and Dr. Dre's Slim Shady Records. But after his sessions with Jay and before he had even released his debut album, he had become a hip hop flavor of the month, receiving heavy radio play and regular video rotation. Word on the street of 50 Cent's skills as an MC first emerged from 24/7.

In fall 2002 Jayson Jackson, a Virgin executive in New York, signed a deal with Jay to distribute a new hip hop act Jay had discovered called Rusty Waters. When Jackson heard the record he immediately liked it and made the deal. Part of the package, of course, was Jay's involvement. "His stamp of approval meant something to us. Jam Master Jay knows music. It was a no-brainer," says Jackson. "Jay was the first guy to recognize how good that guy 50 Cent is. Dj's have good ears." The deal gave Jay an "imprint" at Virgin, or a deal allowing him to produce records that would be sold under his own label. The name he chose for the new venture was Hot Ta Def. Rusty Waters consisted of Jay's pal Randy Allen, who rapped under the name MDR, and Jay's sister's son, Boe Skagz. The Rusty Waters record was nearly done. "All they needed to do was to mix the record and add in a couple more songs," said Jackson.

By the late 1990s the rap-rock revolution that Run-DMC had fostered so many years ago was now returning the favor. Run-DMC's touring began to re-energize and the group went out on the road with Kid Rock and Aerosmith. Of course, in a sense, it was like building it all up from scratch again. They could no longer fill arenas but they could sell out college shows, rock clubs, and small auditoriums. Pretty soon they were back selling out 2,000–5,000-seat auditoriums. And young new audiences weaned on the music of Run-DMC's musical progeny responded wildly to old hits like "Walk This Way" and "King of Rock." Here was a new generation of fans, many of whom had not yet been born when "Sucker MC's" first appeared. Run-DMC was getting new respect, the respect accorded an "old school" act whose legitimacy is still deemed vital.

"Hip hop has always placed a great worth on making connections to a larger historical sense of culture," writes USC Critical Studies professor Todd Boyd in his 2002 book *The New H.N.I.C.* "Thus the lofty status accorded to the idea of an 'old school.' In this regard one is expected to recognize one's origins, and always maintain a strong connection to this history. Not only in terms of one's life and family but also in terms of the music itself. It can also be an acknowledgement of those figures considered estimable within the genre itself or other artists, athletes, or political figures from earlier eras who are deemed appropriate for hip hop culture." Run-DMC fit this description and then some. They were suddenly seen as fathers, as creators of the music these kids loved, and the warmth that flowed out to them was palpable.

Run-DMC was in demand again. Their bookings rose to fifteen or twenty dates a month, a schedule that took them all over the country. DMC's voice was weakened but Run and Jay filled up the space. DMC was so thrilled to be back in action that on a tour of Australia he told a reporter, "We're like, oh, we don't even got to make records to keep our career going, we'll just keep doing this until we're eighty-two years old." And DMC then dropped a little science on the interviewer: "The only reason we lasted so long is because we're doing what was done before hip hop records were made. Forget about the video, forget about the producer, forget about the album, let's see the dj live. My dj's better than your dj. My dj dj's for real, your dj uses a DAT [digital audio tape] and prerecorded tape. We don't rap over no tape."

In 1998 the group got a lift from an unexpected quarter: another dj. That year, American turntablist Jason Nevins released a dance remix of "It's Like That" and it became a smash hit all over Europe. Run-DMC's overseas popularity soared once again and their fee for appearances rose from $20,000 to $50,000, and $70,000 for a large festival. In 2001 Run-DMC performed over 200 shows.

"I am what time, circumstance, and history have made me, certainly, but I am also much more than that. So are we all." James Baldwin wrote those lines forty years ago, but I thought of Jay recently as I read them.

Jay was clearly a product of Hollis in the 1980s, and the hip hop world of the 1980s and 1990s, a representative of its special character. But through his own gentle character he stepped out of the stream of circumstance and hectic daily life and seemed to stand to the side as the world rushed past. When he stood over the grill with his kin at the Mizell family reunions in North Carolina, or took Jason, Terry, and Jesse on a run to the barbershop and back with him on Saturday afternoon, or when he just threw on one of the flannel shirts he kept in the non–hip hop corner of his closet and hung out with Terri for an evening, he was just being Jason Mizell, not Jam Master Jay.

And Jason Mizell was at the crest of one phase in life and looking across the distance toward the next one.

ten

FALLING STAR

> To act is to be committed, and to be committed is to be in danger.
>
> —James Baldwin

On the evening of October 30, Jay was playing a video game with his assistant Uriel Rincon in the lounge of Studio 24/7, when there was a knock on the door. Lydia High, one of Jay's business partners, opened it to see who was there and was immediately pushed to the floor. A man barged in, charged into the lounge, and raised a pistol. By one account Jay saw the gun and tried to duck. He may have screamed out a few words of alarm. But he was too late. The first shot struck Jay in the head, and he went down immediately. As Rincon scrambled to get out of the way, a second shot went wild, hitting him in the leg. For a moment, in the cramped space of the lounge, the shooter collided with Rincon, and they both fell to the floor, toppling furniture with them. The killer jumped to his feet and bolted down the stairwell, out the door, and onto Merrick Boulevard. As he made his escape he may have fled directly past the front door of the 103rd police precinct, which is only a few hundred feet from the studio entrance.

Jam Master Jay died on the spot. The time was 7:30 P.M. It was eleven weeks before his thirty-eighth birthday and just a few months shy of what would have been Run-DMC's twentieth anniversary.

He died wearing a brown leather hat and his white Adidas.

The attack lasted not more than thirty seconds. Randy, Boe Skagz, and Lydia were unscathed. Another assistant, Mike B, who was in the rear room when it happened, saw nothing. The first 911 call came into police just a few minutes later and officers arrived almost immediately. Rain was falling outside, but a crowd began gathering around the studio in a matter of minutes, first drawn by the flashing lights of police cruisers and then by word of mouth. The entire neighborhood began to stir with the horrible news.

Terri Mizell was in her car when the call came on her cell phone. She was driving south to Virginia for a family event. She turned the car around and came back, appearing later at the studio with her stepson Jason, who was crying even as he attempted to comfort his stepmother. Stunned and numb, Terri had a faraway look in her eye, as though she was expecting to awaken any moment with Jay in the safety of her bed, from what must surely be nothing more than a terrible, terrible dream.

"There's no reason," a newspaper quoted Jay's son

Jason later. "He really didn't do anything wrong." DMC was at home in New Jersey when he was awakened by a phone call from Tracey Miller, the group's long-time publicist. He put on his clothes, hopped in his car, and drove toward the studio. Miller had begun working with the group in 1983, just before their big break, and now had the task of delivering the bad news to the Run-DMC family.

Word spread rapidly. The hip hop community is linked by a web of cell phones and instant two-way pagers, and within minutes news of Jay's shooting was leaping from phone to phone and pager to pager, first as a rumor, and then a second time as a grim fact.

Chuck D was at home on Long Island that night. "I heard it on the news. I was just half-listening and then I heard the announcer start giving a history of Run-DMC and I said to myself, 'Oh no, what the hell happened?' At the end of the report he said Jay was dead. I sat there awhile, then I broke out and went down to Merrick Boulevard. It hit me emotionally."

The radio dj Ed Lover was at Madison Square Garden that night when he got the news. "I was at a Knicks game, the first game of the season, and I got a page from somebody saying there is a rumor going around that Jay got shot. I went to Queens right off and I sat out there and watched, and I was just in shock."

DJ Hurricane said it was the worst day of his life. "I got that call and all the air went right out of me. Jay and I came a long way together."

John King was in Florida when he heard it on a

news report. "I just got mad," he said. "Why Jay? There are some people I wouldn't be surprised, but Jay? The guy was like a priest."

Davy D was in Queens that night. "I had just bought a brand-new cell phone and when I turned it on that was the first call I got. Jay's dead."

Kool E said, "I found out the worst way. I was visiting my son in Charlotte and when I got there he met me at the door and said, 'Dad, they killed your man.' He saw it on the Internet."

Rick Rubin was home in Los Angeles when he heard. "I sent Russell Simmons an e-mail immediately saying, 'Please tell me it's not true!' I didn't want to believe it."

Within an hour or so, Def Jam Records bosses Russell Simmons and Lyor Cohen both arrived on the scene, too. "I'm trying to tell myself this isn't true," a shaken and pale Cohen said to a reporter. Outside the studio friends and loved ones from Jay's past and present embraced each other and broke down sobbing. Rappers like to project toughness and invulnerability, but on that night rivers of tears flowed down the faces of some of the toughest men in hip hop. The crowd grew so large that police cordoned off Merrick Boulevard and pushed the throng back behind a line of crime scene tape. For hours the crowd waited there, holding onto the dwindling hope that maybe Jay had survived, that just perhaps the information they were getting was wrong. Maybe somehow he had made it, and would be sitting up in a hospital bed a couple of hours from now joking about it. Jay had been shot before and laughed it off, hadn't he?

At 11:30 P.M. came a sight that no one wanted to see—two New York City Police workers lifted Jay's body down the rear fire escape stairs wrapped in a dark body bag. Jay was loaded into a waiting ambulance and taken to Immaculate Hospital where he was officially ruled dead.

Garfield McDonald had been with Jay earlier that evening. When his cell phone rang later that night he drove straight to the hospital. "I just knew he was all right," Garfield told me as we walked through Hollis in early December. "I was going to walk in and he'd be there. But then they stopped me and told me he didn't make it. I just stood there. I froze. I couldn't believe Jay was gone." Garfield himself had a brush with death in 1986 when a fight broke out in a hotel after a Run-DMC concert and someone fired a shot into a hallway from inside a closing elevator. The bullet struck Garfield in the head and bruised his brain, but he miraculously recovered and walked out of the hospital a week later. More than a month after Jay's death, his face still wears a look of disbelief. All of Hollis was stiller than usual that night.

Over the following days, Studio 24/7 turned into a makeshift shrine. In what has become a familiar routine played out after the sudden death of a media figure—the same sort of gesture seen after the deaths of Princess Diana and John F. Kennedy Jr.—fans made their own pilgrimages to the site of Jay's murder, and long after the scene had fallen still, they deposited candles, flowers, old Run-DMC cd's, and album covers.

One man left a turntable and a pair of white shell-toe Adidas. Despite the rain, the candles burned through most of the night.

One homemade sign read, "Now God has a DJ."

The shock waves of Jay's death rippled around the world. In London, the BBC gave it intensive coverage as did newspapers in Germany, France, Australia, and Japan.

Too many great American stories end with a flash of a gun barrel: Tupac and Biggie, of course, but also John Lennon, Sam Cooke, Marvin Gaye, and even Kurt Cobain. Sudden, violent death has become almost routine in modern America. Jay's death added to the list of talent so egregiously stolen from the public, but it also deprived a wife and mother and three sons of their husband and father.

Still, there was something particularly tragic and galling that the father of modern dj's would die in the studio, the place that was his creative home, his haven, and his favorite place to be, the place where he had helped so many other people chase their dreams.

Jay's death struck a peculiarly sensitive nerve. When Tupac and Biggie were murdered, some critics suggested that their deaths were foretold in their music—as if their words cast a spell that conjured up something evil that had destroyed them. Those murders are still unsolved, so we actually can't yet know why they were killed.

In the aftermath of Jay's death, however, tv pundits and daily newspaper reporters struggled to make sense of the killing. The trouble was it didn't fit into one of the ready-made categories that the media uses in its shorthand analysis of music business deaths. Initially newspapers speculated that the murder was an extension of the East versus West battles that plagued hip hop during the 1990s. There was only one problem with that theory: There was no evidence for it. Jay never engaged in the lyrical battles and insults that fueled the East-West rivalry. Neither did Run-DMC. They rapped about sneakers and fast food and partying with girls, not gats and drive-bys and revenge. While some rappers gin-up rivalries with other rappers as a hook to get curious fans to buy their records, Jay never did so. A second theory soon was floated in newspapers, that Jay was a victim of a drug deal gone bad. That theory took on a life of its own when it was disclosed that Jay died with a large outstanding tax debt—as much as $400,000—owed from his various personal and business ventures. A substantial part of that is believed to have been attached to his studio.

Early in his career when money began flowing in for the first time, he made a mistake common to many people who come into sudden riches: He never sought out financial advice. As early as 1989 he became snared in a web of taxes and penalties that he could never escape from. Perhaps when he was bestowing close friends with gifts of cars and gold chains and buying a dozen of his closest friends champagne for a night, he should have been paying down his taxes. But in a dozen conversations with his close friends and business partners, no one believed that Jay would risk everything he had built—his career, his family, his studio, everything—on something as chancy as a drug deal.

Jay touched on the subject himself in an interview a few years earlier with *NY Talk* magazine. Even "the best crack dealers go to jail," he said. "The guy who makes it on the street is the cool guy. The guy who's got a job and can still dress like this." Most of Jay's friends say his more than abundant street smarts would have kept him clear of any sort of high-stakes gamble like a drug deal, especially when his career was moving so briskly forward. Besides that, they hasten to add, aside from a little marijuana in his younger days, Jay never liked drugs.

Several members of Jay's close friends point to an ongoing dispute Jay had with Queens man by the name of Curtis Scoon that had been simmering for years. As these friends describe it, several years earlier Jay and Scoon each put up $15,000 cash to buy a couple of Rolex watches at a discount price from a contact of Jay's. It turned out to be a scam: The contact disappeared with their money and never delivered the watches. According to Jay's friends, Scoon believed he had been set up—that Jay was somehow in on the rip-off. He demanded that Jay return his money. Jay explained that he had no part in the rip-off, and that he too was out $15,000. But Scoon wasn't buying it. Relations between the two men remained chilly and strained until late 2002, when, say Jay's friends, Scoon began turning up the heat, leaving ominous messages on Jay's phone. In November detectives attempted to interview Scoon but were rebuffed by his lawyer, who insists his client has no connection to the shooting and therefore has nothing to say. "The police have nothing, no evidence on my client," his attorney told me. In late January 2003, police still had not spoken to Scoon. Sources I spoke to in Hollis all strongly doubted that Scoon was the trigger man.

Police also focused on an associate of Scoon's named Ronald Tinard Washington who was arrested December 9, 2002 after allegedly robbing a motel clerk in Long Island. Tinard and Jay were childhood friends; in fact, Tinard is believed to have been one of a group of Jay's junior high school pals who would occasionally hang out at Jay's house listening to records. According to sources in Hollis, in the days after Jay's killing Tinard told anyone who would listen that he was not involved. Tinard's attorney says his client is innocent.

A welter of other theories emerged, too. One centered on the rapper 50 Cent, who cancelled a concert in Philadelphia minutes before he was to go on stage when word reached him of Jay's murder. NYPD offered 50 Cent protection, initially fearing that the one-time protege of Jam Master Jay might be in danger, too, but 50 Cent declined. A few weeks later the New York *Daily News* reported that investigators were looking into the possibility that 50 Cent may have made enemies in the Queens crack trade with a song of his called "Ghetto Qua'ran" that includes references to some of the actual players. The implication, although unsubstantiated, was that enemies of 50 Cent may have shot Jay as a way of retribution against 50 Cent. 50 Cent rarely leaves home without a bullet-proof vest.

In January 2003 an unknown gunman fired six rounds into the front door of the Manhattan office of 50 Cent's management company, Violator Management. 50 Cent was not there at the time, and no one was hit. Investigators told the *New York Post* that a rivalry had sprung up between Violator and Murder Inc., the record label and management company run by Queens native Irv Gotti. When 50 Cent chose to sign with Violator and then Eminem's Shady Record label, reportedly at Jay's suggestion, the *Post* said, it may have triggered a feud between Violator and Murder Inc. That same month, Gotti's offices were raided by federal and NYPD officers looking for connections between Murder Inc. and a Queens drug dealer.

What remains most troubling about Jay's murder are these questions: How did the killer know where to find Jay that night? And presuming that the killing was planned, how could the killer have known that he could enter, shoot Jay without resistance, and escape? Several of Jay's friends strongly suspect that the killer was tipped off by someone watching the studio from the street, or perhaps even by someone inside the studio that evening. Jay's friend Randy Allen told MTV in December that rumors that he was somehow involved in Jay's death were false and outrageous. Some music industry observers say that the federal probe into Murder Inc. is proof that rap music is being infiltrated by former drug dealers drawn by the lure of big money, and that any of a dozen perfectly legal music business deals Jay made in the past five years might have displeased someone comfortable with exercising the strong-arm tactics of the drug world.

On the first Monday after Jay's death, a wake was held at the J. Foster Phillips Funeral Home in Jamaica. Fans stretched along Linden Boulevard for five blocks. Cars rolled by, their radios playing "It's Like That" and "The Avenue." Inside Jay was resting in a black suit, black hat, and his chains. One long-time Queens resident, Jane Mooreman, told *MTV News*: "When I came up here I wanted to go inside because looking at Jay was like watching a son grow up. I'm sixty years old. He grew up with my younger brother. My kids know him. Everybody on the block knows this young man. He inspired everybody."

On the morning of Tuesday, November 5, a white carriage with gold-plated sides drawn by two white horses carried Jay's casket to the Greater Allen Cathedral in Queens, where some 2,500 mourners awaited. Seven pallbearers—including Hurricane and others from the Hollis crew—all wearing black leather jackets, white Adidas, and black velour hats, bore his body into the overpacked church.

Inside, a dozen large funeral wreaths had been placed near the pulpit, including one arranged in the shape of twin turntables. Another spelled out the word

"Hollis." In the front pew sat Terri and the three boys, each wearing sunglasses, a black suit, and a black velour hat.

All of Jay's worlds came together that day. There was the Hollis crew, the guys from the block and the barbershops and the parks who were with him in the beginning, the middle, and the end. There was his half-brother Marvin and his sister Bonita, who still live in the old family house and remembered when Jay first used his parents' stereo to spin 45's.

Of course Run and DMC were there, too. They were the second closest thing he had to brothers, and they were the guys he had spent more time with than anybody. His son Jason's mother, Lee, was there, too, sharing the front row with Terri. Music world VIP's came out in force: rappers Queen Latifah, Busta Rhymes, Chuck D, DMX, Foxy Brown, Treach, Q-Tip, and the Beastie Boys. There were rap executives and managers present: Chris Lighty, Damon Dash, Kevin Lyles, and Jermaine Dupri, and, of course, Russell Simmons and Lyor Cohen. So was the hip hop pioneer Grandmaster Flash, a presence that would undoubtedly have thrilled Jay more so than all the VIP's.

Over the next hour a series of speakers did their best to explain the unexplainable. DMC was one of the first to speak, and he brought the crowd to its feet when he criticized the media for portraying Jay as a hoodlum: "Jam Master Jay was not a thug," DMC began. "Jam Master Jay was not a gangster. He was the embodiment of hip hop. He treated all people like no man was better than the next." McDaniels then rapped a few lines from "Jam Master Jay" and the audience helped him finish the lines.

"He didn't live a long life," said the Reverend Floyd Flake, "but he lived well by the people whose lives he touched." Then, Reverend Run stepped up. Wearing a clerical collar and a broad-brimmed black hat, he followed with some eloquent words for his friend. "He's a builder and his work had been completed," Run intoned. "Let's not ask why Jason is gone. Ask why we are here. Jason helped build hip hop, and his job is finished. I wasn't going to say this," Run continued, "but this is Jay's biggest hit with all the love and support he's getting."

The singer Sparkle delivered an inspirational song and then guests and friends silently filed out of the church into the cool fall air. The funeral procession rolled down Merrick Boulevard, past the studio where Jay's life ended, and just a few blocks from the parks and street corners of Hollis where his amazing journey began.

After the service, many of Jay's friends unburdened themselves of their sadness and rage. "He was one of the kindest-hearted people I met in hip hop. I never seen him raise his voice, always seen him smiling," said the rapper Treach of the group Naughty by Nature.

"This is not superficial starstruck garbage," added Tyrone Williams, founder of the Cold Chillin' record label. "People genuinely loved Jay."

"It's like every year a piece of the puzzle gets taken

away," said the producer Swizz Beatz to *BET.com*. "We lost another pioneer."

Rapper Q-Tip touched on how Jay's success was contagious: "Just for me, growing up in Queens in the same neighborhood, I remember everybody aspiring to be like Jay. We related to them [Run-DMC]. He represented our neighborhood with such pride. If not for them, we probably would not have jobs," he told *Rap Artist Direct*.

Rap executive Steve Rifkind, who founded the very successful Loud Records label in the 1980s, put it quite succinctly: "He was a true gentleman," Rifkind was quoted as saying. "A groundbreaking dj that loved hip hop. He was just a great guy that loved music."

The rapper Nelly remembered that Jay gave him solid advice, not platitudes, when Nelly came to him for pointers early in his career. "Jay was one of the first ones to really come to me and told me to stick to what I was doing," Nelly said to *Launch* online. "He warned me about . . . making the transition of 'crossing over.' When they did 'Walk This Way,' you know, they caught a lot of slack and now you look back and it's a classic."

Writer and former Def Jam publicist Bill Adler told me that "One of the great measures of Jay is that he was working with undiscovered talent on his last day. Most people, including you and I, just don't have a lot of time to be as generous as he was. Somehow Jay always did. That's what people should remember about him."

"When we were down and out and in the depths, Jay and Run and DMC came along and said, 'Come play on our record,' " said the members of Aerosmith in a statement. "Run-DMC and Jam Master Jay's gift to the world was a new kind of music for a whole new generation, and their gift to us was a piece of ourselves back. Jay was scratching before anyone had the itch and still at the top of his game."

In *E! Online* Chuck D said, "You draw the comparison to when John Lennon was shot. It's an enormous loss to the genre." Rapper Pharoahe Monche said to *Rap Artist Direct* that what stings most is that Jay's future has been taken away from him, and fans will never get to see him bask in the recognition he had earned. "It's sad because I wanted to see my hip hop heroes grow old like other musicians."

Ferncliff Cemetery lies off a two-lane road in Westchester County, New York, about a forty-minute drive north of Hollis. With its sprawling grounds, large pond, and immaculate landscaping, it is a soothing oasis of calm set in the densely populated neighborhoods of southern Westchester. It is also the resting place of many great African-American artists and leaders: Malcolm X is buried there. So is the singer Aaliyah, and the great jazz musician Thelonius Monk.

Jam Master Jay was laid to rest there on November 5. His three sons placed roses on his casket as it was lowered into the earth. Then they released white doves into the air.

In an interview in *DJ Times* about a year before he passed, Jay talked about his pride and satisfaction at being on the ground floor of something powerful and good and inclusive. "I like being a part of something that you believe in with your heart and seeing it grow. Now it is the Number One this, the Number One that. And it wasn't just about making hip hop: We were able to make hip hop for everybody."

Not long after Jay's death Russell Simmons commented on hip hop's global power during an interview on National Public Radio. "Jay-Z and Puffy are more popular than Colin Powell around the world," he said. "Puffy's a lot more influential to young people than George Bush. That's a fact. We want to use as much of that influence to push forward positive agendas." Simmons' assertions are difficult to argue with. Hip hop music and videos have conquered the world to a greater extent than even the most aggressive cultural imperialists could ever hope for. Hip hop's journey has indeed been a remarkable one, from basement jams to the voice of a powerful worldwide youth culture. But what is that voice being used to say?

DMC, always the group's reflective spirit, himself wondered that in an interview with MTV shortly before Jay's death. The content of much of the hip hop he was seeing left something to be desired. "It ain't about just the video," he said. "Some of these rappers need to do the same thing [classic rock artists] did, when there's a problem in society or in their community. They would make a record about the Vietnam War. They would make a record about the stuff going on. Everybody thinks because you turn a video on, and you see all the pretty women, and all the pool parties, and the food, and the liquor, and the cars, that everything in the world is fine. The power of communication is the greatest thing that we have, but we ain't teaching that to the young kids. We just teaching them, 'Say a rhyme, get a car, get a big house.' But it's not about that."

In the days following Jay's death, Russell Simmons announced that he was helping to establish a fund that would send the Mizell kids to college and pay off any debts Jay left behind. "Many of us lost a dear friend and an inspiration when Jay was killed. The work of the coalition is to see to it that his family gets the assistance it needs as they try to overcome this tragedy," his statement said. In interviews wherever he went that week Simmons found himself on the defensive, having to remind reporters that Jay's killing was not a sign of a sickness in hip hop, but rather a sign of a greater problem that faces all of society. In a prepared statement, Simmons said the killing "should serve as a reminder of the condition of poverty, ignorance, guns, and lack of opportunity inherent in our urban communities across the country." He dismissed suggestions that gangsta rap's relentless obsession with violence and anger was a cause of the real-life street violence that has claimed hip hop's brightest talent. The music "reflects the environment in which people live. Hopefully the death of Jam Master Jay will remind us all that we need to address the disease plaguing our urban communities and not the symptoms. The hip hop community needs to recommit to talk more about these things."

In a conversation with journalist Nayaba Arinde in the *Final Call* newspaper, dj Ed Lover put more of the responsibility on the industry itself. "We've got to put some love back in this music. This has to be a catalyst to turn this whole business around. We can't censor artists, but we have to instill some love back in their hearts, because hip hop is not reflective of the streets anymore." Rapper Doug E. Fresh agreed that the tone set by the industry can be a powerful force: "The artists, the labels, the executives, the CEO's, we're the leaders, we have to take some responsibility to use our skills to prevent this from ever happening again." Chuck D stressed that rappers ought to use their influence to get tips from the community to find out who committed this crime.

The hip hop world responded strongly: Reward money in the case for information leading to the killer reached $250,000 as contributions from LL Cool J, Dr. Dre, Interscope Records, Eminem, Method Man, Busta Rhymes, Kid Rock, and Aerosmith came in.

In a press conference in the East Room of New York's Righa Royal Hotel, Run called Jay's passing the end of Run-DMC. Going out with another dj was just not acceptable to him, he said, announcing that the ride was over. "Nobody wants to see Run and DMC without Jay. We're not able to go back out with Kid Rock and Aerosmith, and that was a big break for us. Run-DMC is officially retired. We split this money three ways. I can't get out on stage with a new dj." DMC, who was sitting beside him, nodded in agreement. "Some rock bands can replace the drummer but I don't know any other way but with the original three members." That was no surprise because everyone always said Jay was the glue. Now the glue was gone and the band was falling to pieces. The group's eighth album, which was scheduled to have come out in late 2003, is only partly recorded.

As of this writing, in mid-January 2003, no arrests have been made in the murder of Jam Master Jay. There was no evidence left at the scene. A video camera was not operating at the time of the shooting, and the descriptions given by the eyewitnesses were vague, except that the killer is 6' to 6'2" and wore a dark hat. Police removed and examined the studio's computers, pulled phone records, and even took up bits of the studio carpeting as evidence.

There are fears, naturally, that the case could wind up like the killings of Biggie and Tupac: unsolved. Those cases have been hampered by a combination of poor police work and lack of cooperation on the streets. But Charles Fischer, chairman of the Hip Hop Action Network, which is organizing the reward effort and aiding the police investigation, told me that the police are getting "100 percent cooperation from the people of Queens." And Fischer said he has opened a hotline number for citizens with information who are afraid to deal directly with police. Thousands of flyers were printed up and distributed throughout Hollis and

Jamaica telling people where they can send donations to the family, and listing the confidential hotline number.

At the Mizell home on 203rd Street, two days after Jay's death, there was a somber parade of well-wishers coming and going. Large purple ribbons had been hung on the front door. Inside, Jay's sister Bonita was sitting on a couch and weeping. "He stayed here because of me," she said to the *New York Times*. "A long time ago his wife wanted to move out of New York, but he said, 'I'm not leaving my sister.' That's the man he was."

THE SCRATCH GOES ON

History determines whose legacy will endure, and usually many years pass before it makes up its mind. One thing that is clear is that it certainly has little to do with fame or celebrity. The great early-twentieth-century blues guitarist Robert Johnson received scant recognition in his lifetime, made only a few recordings, died broke at an early age, and was buried in an unmarked grave, but Eric Clapton's rendition of Johnson's "Crossroads" helped catapult the British guitarist to fame. Today Johnson's songs are widely covered by some of the most important rock musicians in the world and his music continues to matter. Just a few years ago Columbia Records released a big, expensive multidisc collection of Johnson's original recordings. It sold surprisingly well. His home state of Mississippi even issued a postage stamp bearing his portrait.

Some legacies, however, seem to acquire an enduring sort of significance right from the start.

On a Saturday afternoon in early January, less than three months after Jam Master Jay's death, a gaggle of noisy students is filing into a large sixth-floor loft near the corner of Broadway and Houston Street in New York, right on the border between Greenwich Village and Soho. Class is beginning at the Scratch DJ Academy, and every one of the 180 available spaces is taken. When they're all inside, the students split up—some head to a back room and settle in chairs to listen to a lecture, and others take a position at one of the many turntables arrayed in the front room and get to work.

Over a six-week semester students will receive instruction in scratching, mixing, blending, and beat making, and just about every facet of deejaying you can think of. They will study the history of the dj, probe the inner workings of turntables and tone arms, learn the art of dropping, hear lectures from working dj's, and get advice on how to launch their own careers. Scratch is a dj school, the first of its kind, and marks a giant leap forward for the art form. With a formalized curriculum and hands-on training, the school represents acknowledgment—long overdue some might say—that dj's are in fact musicians, that their turntables are truly instruments, and that the noise they make with them is indeed music.

Scratch is one of Jason Mizell's last projects. He founded it in 2002 with former dot.commer and media exec Rob Principe, and writer Reg E. Gaines, author of the Broadway play *Bring in da Noise, Bring in da Funk*. Principe, twenty-nine, is the Academy's president, and says he got the idea to start up a dj school a few years ago after a night watching a dj electrify a crowded Manhattan party made him suddenly realize that deejaying is a serious, unrecognized art.

"The music was so good, and the dj was so amazing—controlling the mood, making people so enthusiastic—that the experience moved me, just like a movie or a piece of art moves me," Principe told me. He later realized that even though dj's are a permanent part of the music world, so little attention is paid to their considerable technical skill. "You see dj's now in clothing stores and in restaurants and lounges," he said, "they're ubiquitous," but "ask them about how they do what they do and many of them say they've never actually been asked to explain it. What they do isn't getting passed on. You can go to schools for welding and carpentry but no one has formalized what the dj does."

Every art and every culture requires at least three things in order to grow: teachers, students, and texts. Principe understood that in order to get the concept for a dj school out of his notebook and into the real world he'd need to find the best teachers. So he reached out to as many of the top NY dj's as he could find. He got back enthusiastic responses. Two of the biggest stars now teaching at Scratch are Grand Wizard Theodore, the Bronx dj who is widely credited with actually inventing scratching, and DJ Premier, the sonic genius who is also a busy studio producer and half of the hip hop duo Gang Starr.

But to give his start-up more credibility, Principe realized he needed a mainstream personality who could also be the school's informal ambassador. His first choice was Jam Master Jay. "He was the most famous dj in the world and he was right here in New York," said Principe. Principe had met Jam Master Jay once on an airplane some seventeen years ago, when he was twelve and a budding hip hop fan. Their meeting was brief but Principe never forgot Jay's easy charm. So, nearly two decades later, he happened to be in the Green Room of the *Late Night with David Letterman* show and there was Jay, preparing for a live performance with Run-DMC. Principe reintroduced himself and struck up a conversation about deejaying. He then explained his idea for a school that would train kids in the art of the deejaying and send them out into the world. Jay liked the idea, and he loved Principe's sincerity. The two began talking regularly by phone, exchanging ideas, refining their plan. "We decided that the school should provide education and access for people," Principe said. "And Jay saw it as something that would help spread deejaying so it would continue growing after he retired."

Jay, Principe, and Gaines wrote up a curriculum that was several hundred pages long. They codified the theory and the methods that all dj's need to command in order to be effective: mixing, cutting, sustaining a beat, looping, and keeping a flow. "We decided it had to be methodical and scientific. When rock and jazz turned thirty," says Principe, "you could turn on PBS and see them analyzed as serious art forms. There were scholars talking about their development and how they contributed to changes in American culture. We wanted this to happen for dj's, too. The world should know that this is an art form that is coming on fast."

The Academy opened in February 2002 with a handful of students, but only as a lecture series at first because they were without the money to buy equipment. In the spring, in part because of the attention that Jay's association brought and in part thanks to some clever persuasion by Principe and Gaines, the Numark Company donated forty turntables, and the Academy was up and running.

Instruction at Scratch is half theory and half hands-on. Classes are divided into beginners, intermediate, and advanced. For Jay, the Academy became something close to his heart. He came in regularly and taught beginners' classes, carefully taking his students through the history of the dj and then demonstrating some basic turntable moves. He would instantly have a class in the palm of his hand when he explained the function of a dj in terms everyone could relate to: "Anybody who controls music is a dj," he said. "If you're home changing the cd's on your stereo, you're a dj. If you're riding in your car with your friends and picking out cd's, you're a dj. If you're the one choosing the sounds and you have an audience, you're a dj. Everybody is a dj." He told his students how he started deejaying, how he became hooked when he first felt the excitement of seeing an audience hanging on his turntable moves, and experienced the enormous power flowing through his hands.

"He saw it as an honor to teach," Principe recalls. "He was always patient and really wanted kids to learn. He described what he did in detail and then walked around the room to make sure everybody got it. Almost like a carpenter talking about his craft. It was something to see. I said to someone afterwards that learning to dj from Jay was like learning your forehand from John McEnroe." On more than one occasion class spilled over the allotted hour, but Jay always stuck around to take questions and give a little more individual attention if needed. Sometimes he got so wrapped up in teaching that he was late for his next appointment—even if that was a Run-DMC concert.

Saturday, January 11, 2003, was a bittersweet moment at Scratch. It was the first day of a new semester and the first without its founding dj. But two people had come to represent him. In attendance were Jay's two younger sons—Terry and Jesse—who signed up for the coming semester so they could, in a sense, walk in their father's steps.

When all of the students had settled in, Principe stood up and extended them a welcome. He gave a little speech about the history and importance of the dj, and then explained that this was a sad moment because one of the Academy's founders was no longer here. For a moment, the room was dead quiet. Then he continued: "But you guys are carrying on his legacy."

The night before, Terri Corley Mizell had phoned Principe at home to tell him something important. "I want you to know that Jay is very proud," she began. "This is exactly what he wanted. He wanted more than anything to see Scratch grow the way it should. He never talked business at home, but I heard him talking about Scratch a lot. It meant something special to him," she said. "It's keeping alive something that he loved." Jay's brother Marvin phoned, too, to ask if he could come visit the school and maybe share some of his memories of watching a thirteen-year-old Jay spin in the family living room.

There was another honored guest present that day who had phoned up earlier to ask if he could please come and teach something, anything: Darryl McDaniel. DMC was there because he wanted to do something for Jay, he said, something that would keep his projects up and running, and this was one of the first things he thought of. Although DMC's dj credentials don't go much beyond his brief experience twenty years ago in his parents' basement back in Hollis, DMC still remembered a few moves and regaled his DJ 101 class with his thorough knowledge of dj history.

Principe says that the goal he and Jay agreed on was to build the program so it will be strong enough someday to bring to a university music department for accreditation. From there it would spread around the country. Several universities already offer courses in rap, and at least one actually teaches an entire class on the works of Tupac Shakur, but none give advanced dj instruction. "I used to joke with Jay that I was going to make him a visiting professor at Columbia," said Principe. The first batch of Scratch Academy grads received a certificate of completion signed by Jay. Now Principe says they'll have to think up something different. However, what's most important is not a signature but the fact that each student who comes through Scratch is a living part of Jay's legacy.

A week after Scratch's opening, tv audiences got a posthumous look at Jay in a surprising tv commercial that almost didn't happen. Not long before Jay died Run-DMC signed an endorsement contract with the Dr. Pepper soda company to represent the company in a new campaign to reach more ethnic consumers. The vehicle they chose to get there was, of course, hip hop music, and the group they felt best captured hip hop's spirit was Run-DMC. The ad was very nearly pulled after Jay's death, but in early January Terri and Run and DMC and Dr. Pepper all agreed that the ad shows Jay doing what he did best—spinning records and having fun—and carries on his memory in a tasteful way. The ad was broadcast during the NFL playoffs and turned out to be a big hit with viewers. Its success raised the possibility that Run-DMC's breakup may not be final at all, and that perhaps at the right time,

Run and DMC might take to the road again in honor of Jay.

"The world is before you and you need not take it or leave it as it was when you came in," James Baldwin once wrote. Jay did not take the world as he found it and he left it far better off than it was when he entered. Although his time was short, he achieved more than most of us will ever accomplish, even with far more time to work with. Jay flew through life, and he did so not just with speed but with grace. Young men in a hurry often think they're special. Usually they're not. It's those who see their talent as a gift, not an entitlement to power or personal privilege, who change the world in ways that count. Years from now, when music historians look back across the decades to understand how hip hop changed America, inevitably the trail will lead them to Jay. His musical legacy is so large as to be almost incalculable. It was already firmly established before he passed away. Jay provided much of the raw material that the mainstream gobbled up.

The modern sound of the music—edgy, aggressive, uncompromising, beat-oriented—flowed directly out of his turntable. And that most fundamental development of all—the alignment of hip hop with the raw, rambunctious energy of the street—was the master stroke that gave the music a bottomless mystique, and captured the curiosity of the world. That, too, has Jay's signature on it. He was there at the creation of rap-rock, which is now one of the main branches of pop music. And of course, the worldwide primacy of the turntable—which is this generation's equivalent of the guitar—owes so much to Jay. The widely copied sartorial style that was born with the music—from the Adidas and the leather jackets to the black velour hats that defined the look of modern hip hop—came straight out of Jay's closet.

The joining of hip hop with corporate America—linking Hollis Avenue with Madison Avenue, a connection now worth billions, took its first steps in Jay's Adidas. So too, did the concept of hip hop as not merely entertainment, but lifestyle. This realization is what enabled entrepreneurs who recognized how widely Jay's style was imitated—businessmen like P. Diddy of Bad Boy Records and Damon Dash of the Roc-A-Fella Records conglomerate—to extend their record label brands into apparel lines with sales of $100 million per year. The sweet spot that hip hop found in the hearts and wallets of America's youth carried it from a sideshow onto the main stage of America's pop cultural life. Much, if not all, of the DNA of the modern hip hop nation comes from Jay.

In the hip hop nation there is no constitution, but there are founding fathers; there is no Bible but there is a very real and active spirit. Jay was a father of the genre, to be sure, but perhaps his most important gift was the gift of his heart.

In the quiet space between Run and DMC's amusingly loud-mouthed bravado and in the silent halfnotes between Jay's blasting beats there was palpable delight in the art of creating hip hop. There was something optimistic in the idea that the communal experience of this music would make them, their listeners, and their world all better. In that sense their music was their mission.

For Jay the music was the foundation of everything he built, but what the music allowed him to do in the bigger world was where one could find the true meaning of his life. Every time he greeted a fan with a smile instead of a scowl, every time he surprised someone close to him with an expensive gift, every time he opened up his studio or landed a pal a money-making gig or took twenty-five buddies in through the VIP door of a concert behind him, he was giving flesh to the generosity of spirit that he saw as the essential significance of hip hop.

Hip hop started off as mere entertainment, but Jay quickly realized its power and responsibility. Hip hop wasn't about conspicuous consumption and mansions and excess and accumulation. In the end, the gold chains were just a prop, a piece of theater to grab the public's attention. It was just a part of the song; it was not the singer. Jay located hip hop's heart in a solid altruism that stood behind all the tough posing and rough edges. That altruism formed the backbone that held together everything he did. What good is the power or the money if you don't know how to use it, he seemed to understand. What good is it if it doesn't bring out the best in you and help you better the world?

* * *

Can a single gunshot turn a life of victories into a tragedy?

In the days after Jay passed away, the Mizell family experienced an extraordinary outpouring of gratitude and love. The number of people who came forward with anecdotes telling how Jay had given so much to them or left an indelible mark on their life was an extraordinary testament to a life well lived. A college fund was set up for his children, and record executives and friends vowed to pay off the mortgage on Terri and Jay's home. As Terri greeted and mourned with Jay's old friends and family, giving each of them a hug and a reassuring word, you could tell by the way she held on to them, the way her embrace lingered for just a moment, that she could feel a little bit of Jay's spirit in each of them.

His turntables have fallen still, but if you look around hip hop today, he left behind a world of people who loved him, and a world of music forever changed; that is indeed a legacy.

At the 2002 Billboard Awards in Las Vegas in November, the long show climaxed in a tribute to Jam Master Jay. Nelly, Aerosmith, Busta Rhymes, and a stage full of performers delivered a rowdy performance of "Walk This Way." Then, in one of her first public appearances since Jay's death, a very poised Terri Corley Mizell took the stage. The audience hushed.

"Since Jay passed, it has been so hard," she began, looking out at the crowd of 15,000 and a vast tv audience. "But I just had fun tonight. Thanks for your love and continuous support. If Jason were here he'd be so happy. He would have been amazed to see all this love. I don't think he really understood the love and affection his fans had for him."

The roar of affirmation that rose up from the hall signaled just how much the fans were with her. Terri went on to say that she is saving all the notes of sympathy that came pouring in after Jay's death, so in the future her children can read them and will always know what their father meant to the world.

What did Jam Master Jay mean to the world? The rhythm of his music was the pulse of hip hop, and Jam Master Jay was hip hop's heart.

About the Author

David Thigpen is a correspondent on staff at *Time* magazine. From 1993 to 2000 he was a New York–based pop-music writer, covering hip hop, rock, and jazz, and contributed to the magazine's milestone "Hip-Hop Nation" cover story. Thigpen's work has also appeared in the *New York Times*, *People* magazine, and *Rolling Stone*. He is currently based in *Time*'s Chicago bureau, and is married to Veronica Anderson.